Princes and Po

Studies of the Court of I

Frantz Funck-Brentano
(Translator: George Maidment)

Alpha Editions

This edition published in 2024

ISBN 9789362095084

Design and Setting By

Alpha Editions

www.alphaedis.com

Email - info@alphaedis.com

As per information held with us this book is in Public Domain.
This book is a reproduction of an important historical work.
Alpha Editions uses the best technology to reproduce historical work
in the same manner it was first published to preserve its original nature.
Any marks or number seen are left intentionally to preserve.

Contents

PREFATORY NOTE

TWELVE months ago I had the honour of introducing M. Frantz Funck-Brentano to the English public by my translation of his *Légendes et Archives de la Bastille*, and in my preface to that book I gave a rapid sketch of his career which need not be repeated. If history is to be continually reconstructed, or rather, perhaps, to undergo a process of destructive distillation, there is no one more competent than M. Funck-Brentano to perform the feat. We lose our illusions with our teeth; the fables that charmed our childhood dissolve in the modern historian's test-tube, and the mysteries that fascinated our forebears become clear with a few drops of his critical acid.

In his former book, M. Funck-Brentano solved once for all the mystery of the Man in the Iron Mask, showed up the impostor Latude in his true colours, and gave us surprising information about the latter days of the Bastille. In the present volume, the fruit of several years' research among the archives at the Arsenal Library, he conclusively dispels the cloud of suspicion that has hung over the sudden death of Charles I's winsome and ill-fated daughter Henrietta; gives us for the first time the authentic history of that beautiful poisoner Madame de Brinvilliers; suggests a very plausible explanation of Racine's hitherto inexplicable retirement from dramatic writing; and throws a strange light upon the private history of Madame de Montespan and other fair ladies of Louis XIV's Court. If it be objected that some of the details of the 'black mass' and kindred abominations are too gruesome for print, it may be urged in reply that these details are related with the cold impartial pen of a serious historian, not coloured or heightened with a view to melodramatic effect. 'Truth's a dog that must to kennel,' says Lear's Fool; Louis the Magnificent tried to stifle the damning evidence against his jealous, passionate mistress; when Time and patient research among long-forgotten papers have combined to bring the truth to light, it would ill become us to blame a scholar like M. Funck-Brentano for not joining the monarch's conspiracy of silence.

G. M.

November 1900.

MARIE MADELEINE DE BRINVILLIERS

I. HER LIFE

IN the judicial annals of France there has never been a more striking or celebrated figure than the Marquise de Brinvilliers. The enormity of her crimes, the brilliance of her rank, the circumstances accompanying her trial and death,—the story of which, as told by her confessor, the abbé Pirot, is one of the masterpieces of French literature,—finally, the strange energy of her character, which after her execution caused her to be regarded as a saint by a portion of the population of Paris: all these things will for long years to come attract to her the attention of all who are interested in the history of the past.

Michelet devoted to the Marquise de Brinvilliers a study in the *Revue des Deux Mondes*. But his story is very inaccurate and leaves many gaps. From the historical point of view, the little novel of Dumas is much to be preferred. The beautiful criminal has also been dealt with by Pierre Clément in his *Police of Paris under Louis XIV*, and more recently by Maître Cornu, in his discourse at the reopening of the lecture-term of the advocates to the Court of Cassation. The writer of the following pages has been able to make use of some fresh documents.

In the trial of the Marquise de Brinvilliers there is much to interest the historian. It was the first of the terrible poison cases which caused such a sensation at the court of Louis XIV in the central years of his reign, and in which the greatest names in France were implicated; and Madame de Brinvilliers herself represents the most salient and most easily studied features of a type of woman which, as we shall see, repeated itself after her even on the steps of the throne.

Marie Madeleine—and not Marguerite—d'Aubray, Marquise de Brinvilliers, was born on July 22, 1630. She was the eldest of the five children of Antoine Dreux d'Aubray, lord of Offémont and Villiers, councillor of state, *maître des requêtes*, civil lieutenant of the city, mayoralty, and viscounty of Paris, and lieutenant-general of the mines of France. Dreux d'Aubray was himself the son of a treasurer of France, originally from Soissons. Madeleine d'Aubray received a good education, in a literary point of view at any rate. The spelling of her letters is correct, a rare thing with the ladies of her time. Her handwriting is remarkable: bold, firm, like a man's, and such as the observer would be disposed to ascribe to an earlier period. But her religious education was entirely neglected. At her interviews with her confessor on the eve of her death she displayed an utter ignorance of the most elementary maxims of religion,—those which people learn as children, and never during the whole course of their life forget.

Of moral principles she was absolutely destitute. From the age of five she was addicted to horrible vices. At seven she was only by courtesy a maiden. These are what Michelet calls 'a young girl's peccadilloes.' As time went on, she yielded herself to her young brothers. On these points her own testimony renders mistake impossible. She will show herself to have been endowed with an ardent, affectionate nature, which gave her passions command of an amazing energy; but this energy acted only under the empire of her passions, for she was powerless to resist the impressions which penetrated and ere long dominated her. She was extremely sensitive to affronts, and particularly to those which touched her pride. She was one of those natures which under good guidance are capable of heroic deeds, but which are also capable of the greatest crimes when they are wholly abandoned to evil instincts.

In 1651, at the age of one-and-twenty, Marie Madeleine d'Aubray wedded a young officer of the Norman regiment, Antoine Gobelin de Brinvilliers, baron of Nourar, the son of a president of the audit office. He was a direct descendant of Gobelin, the founder of the celebrated manufacture. Mademoiselle d'Aubray brought her husband a dowry of 200,000 livres, and as he too was wealthy, the young couple enjoyed what was for that time a large fortune.

The young marchioness was charming—a pretty, sprightly woman, with large expressive eyes. She made a great impression by her frank, decided, and vivacious manner of speaking. She was of an amiable and cheerful temperament, and dreamed of nothing but pleasure. A priest endowed with great keenness of judgment, who studied the Marquise de Brinvilliers in terrible circumstances, has described her as follows:—

'She was naturally intrepid and of a great courage. She appeared to have been born with inclinations towards good, with an air of complete indifference, with a keen and penetrating intellect, forming clear views of things, and expressing them in words few and fit but very precise; wonderfully ready in finding expedients for getting out of a difficulty, and quick to make up her mind upon the most embarrassing questions; frivolous, moreover, with no application, uneven and inconstant, becoming impatient if the same subject were often talked about.

'Her soul had something naturally great—a composure in face of the most unexpected emergencies, a firmness that nothing could move, a resolution to await and even suffer death if need be.

'She had thick and beautiful chestnut hair, with comely and well-rounded features—her eyes blue, tender, and of perfect beauty, her skin extraordinarily white, her nose well-shaped enough; nothing in her countenance was unpleasing.

'Sweet as her face naturally appeared, when some vexatious idea crossed her imagination she showed it plainly by a grimace that might at first sight scare you; and from time to time I noticed contortions that bespoke disdain, indignation, and scorn.

'She was of a very slight and dainty figure.'

To the Marquis de Brinvilliers luxury and large expenditure had become second nature; he loved gaming and pleasure generally; and his marriage was very far from banishing his joyous habits. In 1659 he formed a close intimacy with a certain Godin, known more often as Sainte-Croix, a captain of horse in the Tracy regiment, originally from Montauban, and said to be a by-blow of a noble Gascon family. Sainte-Croix was young and handsome; 'endowed,' says a memoir of the time, 'with all the advantages of intelligence, and perhaps, too, with those qualities of heart under whose empire a woman rarely fails, in the long-run, to fall.' In after days, Maître Vautier had to sketch the portrait of Sainte-Croix in the course of an address before the Parlement. 'Sainte-Croix,' he said, 'was in poverty and distress, but he had a rare and singular genius. His countenance was prepossessing, and gave promise of intelligence. Such indeed he had, and of such sort as to give universal pleasure. He took his pleasure in the pleasure of others; he entered into a religious scheme as joyfully as he accepted the suggestion of a crime. Keenly sensitive to insult, he was susceptible to love, and in love jealous to madness, even of persons on whom public debauchery assumed rights that were not unknown to him. His extravagance was amazing, and supported by no occupation; for the rest, his soul was prostituted to every form of crime. He dabbled also in external piety, and it has been claimed that he wrote devotional books. He spoke divinely of the God in whom he did not believe, and favoured by this mask of piety, which he never removed save with his friends, he appeared to participate in good deeds while really immersed in crime.' Though he was an officer and married, Sainte-Croix sometimes assumed the garb and the title of Abbé.

Sainte-Croix was a brilliant and gallant cavalier; and the Marquise de Brinvilliers, with her blue eyes and dainty figure, was the most charming creature in the world. 'Lady Brinvilliers,' observes Vautier the advocate, 'did not make a mystery of her amour; she gloried in it in society, whence there resulted much éclat.' She gloried in it also before her husband, who responded by boasting of his own love for other ladies; but as she ventured also to brag about it before her father, the civil lieutenant, a man of the old school, he, strong in the rights with which ancient customs endowed a father, obtained a *lettre de cachet* against his daughter's lover. On March 19, 1663, Sainte-Croix was arrested 'in the marquise's own carriage as he sat by her side,' and was thrown into the Bastille.

Various writers who have dealt with these facts depict Sainte-Croix as the prison companion of the famous Exili, from whom he learnt the secret of Italian poisons. Restored to liberty, Sainte-Croix is said to have handed the terrible prescriptions to his mistress and others, who in their turn spread them through France.

We find this opinion expressed in the documents of the time, among others in the speech delivered by Maître Nivelle before the Parlement, on behalf of Madame de Brinvilliers.

Exili, whose real name was Eggidi or Gilles, was an Italian gentleman attached to the service of Queen Christina of Sweden. It is true that he was confined in the Bastille at the same period as Sainte-Croix. He remained there from February 2 to June 27, 1663; Sainte-Croix was there from March 19 to May 2. A captain of police named Desgrez—who will play an important part in the sequel—met Exili on leaving prison with an order to conduct him to Calais and embark him for England; but, whether Exili gave him the slip on the way, or that he had no sooner reached England than he returned to France, we soon find the Italian again in Paris, and in the house of Sainte-Croix himself, with whom he stayed for six months. After all, it was not Exili who trained Sainte-Croix in the 'art of poisons,' to adopt the phrase of the time. Long before he entered the Bastille the young cavalry officer had acquired a knowledge of poisons which far exceeded that of Exili. He owed it to a celebrated Swiss chemist named Christophe Glaser, who had set up an establishment in the Faubourg Saint-Germain, where he had attained a considerable standing, after the publication in 1665 of a *Treatise on Chemistry*, which had a noteworthy success at the time, and was often reprinted and translated. Glaser was apothecary in ordinary to the king and Monsieur,[1] and demonstrator in chemistry to the Jardin des Plantes. He was, moreover, a scientist of real merit. Sulphate of potassium, which he discovered, long bore his name. Glaser was the principal, probably the only person who furnished Sainte-Croix and his mistress with poisons. In their correspondence the two lovers call the poisons which they used 'Glaser's recipe.' These poisons, however, as we shall see, were very simple; in these days they would appear clumsy. Exili, who goes out of our story, remained connected with Queen Christina, and in 1681 made an excellent marriage when he wedded the Countess Ludovica Fantaguzzi, cousin of Duke Francis of Modena.

As soon as Sainte-Croix left the Bastille he renewed his relations with the Marquise de Brinvilliers. Her passion had only been heightened by the imprisonment of her lover. Wounded in her pride, she felt the birth within herself of an implacable and violent hatred of her father. Her dissipations, her gaming, her wild flings in her lover's company (she paying expenses, after the fashion of that period), had embarrassed her fortune. 'I accuse myself,' she said in her confession, 'of having given a great deal of my wealth to this man, and he ruined me.' The desire of attaining possession of her paternal inheritance, and the yearning, growing day by day more imperious, for wreaking vengeance on her father for the affront put upon her, suggested to her a frightful crime. There might frequently have been seen, drawing up at the market-square of Saint-Germain, a carriage from which alighted a young officer and a fashionable lady. They went on foot to the Rue du Petit-Lion, in which Glaser the chemist lived. Arrived at his house, they sought a retired room. The neighbours, puzzled by these strange goings-on, spoke of false money. Soon this young lady might have been seen, under the edifying appearance of piety and religion, going into the hospitals; she bent over the beds of the patients with words of gentleness and affection; she carried them confections, wine, and biscuits; but the patients whom she approached inevitably succumbed, ere long, in horrible anguish. 'Who would have dreamt,' writes Nicolas de la Reynie, the lieutenant of police, 'that a woman brought up in a respectable family, whose form and constitution were delicate and who in appearance was sweet-natured, would have made an amusement of going to the hospitals to poison the patients, for the purpose of observing the different effects of the poison she gave them?' She poisoned her own servants, too, 'to try experiments.' 'Françoise Roussel says that she has been in the service of Lady Brinvilliers. The latter one day gave her some preserved gooseberries to eat, on the point of a knife, and soon afterwards she felt ill; she gave her also a moist slice of ham, which she ate, and since then she has had severe abdominal pains, feeling as though her heart were being stabbed.' The poor woman was ill for three years.

When the marquise had tested the strength of 'Glaser's recipe,' and had noted the inability of the surgeons to discover traces of poison in the corpses, the poisoning of her father was resolved on.

As Whitsuntide drew on in the year 1666, Antoine Dreux d'Aubray, who had been suffering for some months from strange disorders, set out for his estates at Offémont, a few leagues from Compiègne. He asked his daughter to bring her children and spend a few weeks with him, and when she arrived he scolded her affectionately for having been so long in coming. On the day after her arrival his sickness was redoubled; 'he had great vomitings, continuing with increasing violence till his death,' which occurred at Paris, whither he had himself transported in order to secure the services of the best physicians, and whither his daughter had not failed to accompany him. Madeleine de Brinvilliers confessed afterwards that she had poisoned her father twenty-eight or thirty times with her own hands, and at other times by the hands of a lackey named Gascon, presented to her by Sainte-Croix. The poison was given both in water and in powder, and the process lasted eight months. 'She could not manage it,' she said. It is clear that the poison she employed was simply arsenic. When in the course of time the facts were known, all Europe clamoured with indignation at the thought of this woman heaping caresses on her dying father, and responding to his embraces by pouring poison into the medicines she handed him with her engaging smile. 'The greatest crimes,' said Madame de Sévigné, 'are a mere trifle in comparison with being eight months poisoning her father and receiving all his caresses and tendernesses, to which she replied by doubling the dose. Medea was nothing to her.'

D'Aubray died at Paris on September 10, 1666, aged sixty-six years. The physicians who made an autopsy of the body attributed death to natural causes; but the rumour at once got abroad that he had died of poison. The elder brother of the marquise, whose name was the same as his father's, succeeded him in the family estates and the office of civil lieutenant.

Delivered thus from a formidable censor, Madame de Brinvilliers no longer put any restraint on her debaucheries. She had several lovers at once, in addition to Sainte-Croix. By him she had 'two children among her own'; she was the mistress of F. de Pouget, Marquis de Nadaillac, captain of light horse, and cousin of her husband. Another lover was a cousin of her own, by whom she had a child. Finally, she granted her favours to a mere youth, her children's tutor, of whom there will be much more to say. In spite of this, she felt keenly irritated when Sainte-Croix appeared to be unfaithful to her; and when she learnt that her husband was keeping a woman named Dufay, in her rage she thought of stabbing her. 'She had naturally a great delicacy of feeling,' her confessor was to write of her, 'and was highly sensitive on a point of honour and in regard to injuries.'

Her expenses and prodigalities redoubled, and it was not long before her share of her father's wealth had melted away. At this point occurs an incident which bears witness at once to the distress into which she had fallen and to the savage energy of her character. In 1670, a property belonging to herself and her husband at Norat, was sold by order of the Court to satisfy their creditors; in her ungovernable fury the marquise attempted to set the place on fire.

The greater part of her father's estate had come to her two brothers, one of whom had been appointed civil lieutenant, as we have seen; the other was councillor to the Court. Madame de Brinvilliers had already tried to procure the assassination of the elder by two hired bravoes on the road to Orleans—one of those audacious strokes which to the end of her days she never ceased to devise. She declared at this moment that her brother was 'no good.' Pressed by need of money, she 'resolved on fresh poisonings so as not to lose the fruits of the first.' Sainte-Croix was fully agreed as to the necessity of the proceedings; but before he set about carrying them into effect he got from his mistress two promissory notes, one for 25,000, the other for 30,000 livres.

In 1669, Madame de Brinvilliers succeeded in introducing a wretch named Jean Hamelin, commonly known as La Chaussée, into her brother the councillor's household as a footman. The two brothers lived in the same house, and La Chaussée had every facility for giving poison to both. One day when he was waiting at table, the dose he put into the glass he was handing was so strong that the civil lieutenant rose up in great agitation, crying, 'Ah, wretch, what have you given me? I think you want to poison me!' And he bade his secretary taste the stuff. The latter took some on a spoon and declared that he detected a strong taste of vitriol. La Chaussée did not lose his head. 'No doubt it is the glass Lacroix (the valet) used this morning,' he said, 'when he took medicine.' And he hastily threw the contents of the glass into the fire.

The civil lieutenant went to his estate at Villequoy in Beauce, to spend Easter with his family. In 1670 Easter fell on April 6. His brother the councillor made one of the party, and took La Chaussée with him as his only attendant. While they stayed at Villequoy La Chaussée helped in the kitchen. One day a tart came to table, of which all who ate were very ill on the morrow, while the others remained quite well. On April 12 they returned to Paris, and the civil lieutenant had the appearance of a man who had suffered great pain.

The details of the poisoning are horrible. As D'Aubray did his best to restore his health, the poison did not take effect so quickly as usual; he was very difficult to kill. La Chaussée, assiduous in his attentions, gave his master poison at every possible opportunity. His body was so offensive during his illness that it was impossible to remain in the room with him; and he was so irritable that no one could approach him. Madame de Brinvilliers rarely showed herself, but sent her pious sister to take her place. Meanwhile La Chaussée was unremitting in his care; no one but him could change the bedclothes or the mattress. The unhappy man suffered unspeakable torture. La Chaussée could not help exclaiming: 'This fellow holds out well! He's giving us a good deal of trouble! I don't know when he will give up the ghost!'

Madame de Brinvilliers was at Sains in Picardy. She told Briancourt, the tutor who had become her lover, that the poisoning of her brother the councillor was in progress. She explained to him that she wanted to set up 'a good house'; that her eldest son, who was already nicknamed the President, would one day fill the post of civil lieutenant, and added that 'there was still a good deal to be done.' These sentiments were sincere. Madame de Brinvilliers endeavoured to bring up and establish her children—'who were her own flesh,' as she said—in conformity with the brilliant dreams she nourished for the future of her 'house.' True, she began to poison her eldest daughter, but that was because she thought her a ninny. She was seized with regret, however, and made her drink milk as an antidote.

Such was one of her dominant preoccupations. To this must be added her longing to live with 'honour,' that is, with a brilliant household, with beautiful ornaments, keeping up a great style, and entertaining her lovers with magnificence. She longed for 'the glory of the world,' a phrase continually on her lips. It was for 'honour' that she poisoned so many people. Such was her own statement.

The martyrdom of her brother the civil lieutenant lasted three months. 'He grew thin,' declares his physician, 'and emaciated; lost his appetite, often vomited, and had burning pains in the stomach.' He died on June 17, 1670. The councillor died in the following September. In this case, Dr. Bachot, the civil lieutenant's usual attendant, along with surgeons Duvaux and Dupré and the apothecary Gavart, declared after an autopsy that the deceased had been poisoned; but so little were the perpetrators of the crime suspected that La Chaussée drew a hundred crowns left him by his master as a reward for his faithful service.

We must follow the career of the marquise after the poisoning of her father and brothers, to understand to what depths her ill-regulated passion had thrown this woman, who belonged to the highest ranks of society by her name, her fortune, and the position of her family, and who was so charmingly endowed by Nature.

She was at the mercy of a lackey, who held her honour and her life in his miserable hands. 'She used to receive him privately in her sitting-room, where she gave him money, saying, "He is a good fellow, and has done me great service"; and she caressed him.' Visitors coming upon her unawares found the marquise 'in great familiarity with La Chaussée,' and 'she made him hide behind her bed when the Sieur Cousté came to see her.'

Sainte-Croix was a more formidable accomplice. What must have been the agony of this proud and passionate woman when she understood little by little that this man, to whom she had sacrificed everything, had seen in her only an instrument of his own pleasure and fortune, and now profited by his mastery of her secrets to squeeze money out of her by the most vulgar methods of intimidation! Sainte-Croix had locked up in a small box, which was to become famous, the letters, thirty-four in number, sent him by the marchioness, the two promissory notes signed by her after the murder of her father and brothers, and several bottles of poison. 'The said Lady Brinvilliers coaxed Sainte-Croix to give her his box, and wished him to give her her note for two or three thousand pistoles; otherwise she would have him poniarded.' The woman speaks out in this last phrase. At other times, desperate, frantic with terror, she thought of poisoning herself. She implored Sainte-Croix to give her the box, and when she received no answer, sent him this touching note: 'I have thought it best to put an end to my life, and I have therefore taken this evening what you gave me at so dear a price—the recipe of Glaser; by which you will see that I have willingly sacrificed my life to you; but I do not promise you, before I die, that I will not await you somewhere to bid you a last farewell.' In the last line she becomes herself again; there you have the menace of the offended woman.

What scenes for a romancer to write! One day, by way of reply to these cries of blood, Sainte-Croix made her swallow poison. It was arsenic; but the pain she felt warned her immediately, and she absorbed great quantities of warm milk and so saved herself. She was ill from the effects for several months. She declared after the death of Sainte-Croix 'that she had done what she could to get the box from him while he was alive, and if she had succeeded, she would afterwards have cut his throat.'

Like all criminals, Madame de Brinvilliers was dominated by the unconquerable impulse to lead the conversation continually to the subject of her crimes. She would talk about poisons to any one she met. Her servants found bottles of arsenic in her dressing-room. One day, when very merry—she had taken too much wine—she went up to her room carrying a sort of casket in her hand, and meeting one of her servants told her 'that she had the wherewithal to wreak vengeance on her enemies, and that there were many inheritances in that box'—a terrible phrase which was repeated at her trial and became a catchword; poison was called afterwards 'powder of inheritance.' 'When she came to her senses shortly afterwards the marquise told her servant that she did not know what she was saying when she spoke of inheritances, and that her troubles were sending her out of her mind.' She fancied that she had also betrayed herself before her maid,

Mademoiselle de Villeray, and it is possible that in 1673, to secure her silence, she poisoned her too.

Little by little she came to reveal her crimes in all their details to Briancourt. In the course of her conversations with him, she displayed no regret at the death of her brothers, whom she despised, but she often wept when speaking of her father. 'On the morning after one of these confidences,' said Briancourt before the judges, 'the Marquise de Brinvilliers rushed into my room like a madwoman, and told me that she much mistrusted me, having confided to me matters of the utmost consequence, in which her life was involved. I told her that I would never speak of the things confided to me, but I begged her, with tears in my eyes, that if she was not satisfied with my conduct she would allow me to return to Paris. The lady replied: "No, no,—if you will only be discreet; I will make your fortune, and I am sure of your discretion." About the same time the lady fetched Sainte-Croix back, and they held long conversations together. He showed me the greatest marks of friendliness, assuring me of his services, and begged me to watch over the little boy, of whom he was fond.' We know by Madame de Brinvilliers' own confession that this little boy was actually Sainte-Croix' child.

This deposition of Briancourt constitutes one of the most curious documents in our possession. This man was well disposed and at heart upright, but lacked backbone. His terrible mistress ruled and awed him. Yet he had flashes of that boldness into which feeble natures are occasionally drawn. After having poisoned her father and brothers the marquise had still to get rid of her sister, Thérèse d'Aubray, and her sister-in-law, Marie Thérèse Mangot, widow of the civil lieutenant. That is what 'remained to be done.' 'Seeing the imminent peril of Mademoiselle d'Aubray and even of Madame d'Aubray (though the widow's danger was not so near as the younger lady's), and because La Chaussée had not yet entered the house of Madame d'Aubray, and Madame de Brinvilliers said that she wished the widow's business to be managed in two months or not at all, he (Briancourt) begged the marquise to take care what she was at, said that she had cruelly put her father and brothers to death and wished to do the same with her sister; that he had never come upon an example of such cruelty in all the annals of antiquity, and that she was the cruelest and wickedest woman that ever had been or would be; that he begged her to reflect on what she meant to do, and to remember how that wretch Sainte-Croix had ruined her and her family; that he saw no safety for her, but sooner or later she would perish; that he himself would never allow the murder of Mademoiselle d'Aubray, even though she had once written to Madame de Brinvilliers a letter in which she accused him of being a rogue and rake.' It was unquestionably Briancourt's attitude which saved the lives of Madame de Brinvilliers' sister and sister-in-law; he had further warned Mademoiselle d'Aubray, through the marquise's maid Mademoiselle de Villeray, to be on her guard. In her confession the marquise declared that if she had thought of poisoning her sister it was out of hatred, by way of revenge for remarks she had made to her about her conduct.

Briancourt had only succeeded in diverting the peril upon himself. Madame de Brinvilliers resolved to rid herself of a lover who responded to her confidences by playing the censor. The customary means, poison, was obviously the first to suggest itself. 'Sainte-Croix,' says Briancourt, 'had introduced into the Brinvilliers household a porter related to La Chaussée, and a lackey named Bazile, who was extraordinarily assiduous in serving me with food and drink; but seeing these attentions and, further, some sign of roguery in this fellow, I handled him so roughly that Madame de Brinvilliers had to dismiss him.'

There followed a remarkably romantic scene, as Briancourt described it before the court.

'Two or three days after Bazile's departure, Lady Brinvilliers told me that she had a very handsome bed, and hangings embroidered to match; that it was a bed which Sainte-Croix had pawned and which she had redeemed. She had it put up in her large room, where there was a close and wainscoted chimney-piece, and told me that I must come that night and sleep in that bed, and that she would expect me at midnight, but that I must not come earlier, because she had to arrange with her cook. Instead of going down at midnight to a gallery which commanded the windows of the room, I came down at ten o'clock, and looking through the windows into the room, the curtains not being drawn, I saw the lady walking up and down and dismissing all her servants.'

We may remark in passing that this gallery still exists at the present day in the mansion inhabited by Madame de Brinvilliers in the Rue Neuve-Saint-Paul.[2]

'About half-past eleven,' continues Briancourt, 'Lady Brinvilliers, having undressed and put on her dressing-gown, took a few turns in the room, holding a torch in her hand; then she went to the chimney-piece, which she opened. Sainte-Croix stepped out, dressed in rags, with a worn-out jerkin and an old hat, and kissed the lady, and for a quarter of an hour they talked together. Then Sainte-Croix went back into the chimney-piece, and the lady pushed its two folding-doors to, so as to shut him in, and then came to the door, in some agitation; my own agitation was no less. Should I enter, or should I go away? But the lady seeing my confusion said: "What is the matter? Don't you want to come?" I saw much rage in her countenance, which was changed in an extraordinary degree. I went into the room, and the lady asked me if the bed was not very fine; I said that it was, and the lady rejoined, "Let us lie down then." Then the marquise got into bed. I had placed the torch on a stand, and she said, "Undress yourself and put out the light very quickly." I pretended to be undoing my shoes, desiring to know how far the lady's cruelty would go, and she said, "What is the matter with you? You look very solemn." Then I rose and, giving the bed a wide berth, said to the lady: "Ah, how cruel you are! What have I done that you want to have me murdered?" The lady sprang out of bed and flung herself upon me from behind; but freeing myself, I went straight to the chimney-piece. Sainte-Croix came out, and I said to him: "Ah, villain, you have come to stick a knife into me!" and as the torch was burning, Sainte-Croix made to flee, while Lady Brinvilliers rolled on the floor declaring that she would live no longer, but die; at the same time she sought her case of poisons, opened it, and was on the point of taking poison. I prevented her and said, "You wanted to get me poisoned by Bazile, and now you want to get me stabbed by Sainte-Croix." The lady threw herself at my feet, declaring that such had not happened to me and would never happen, and that she would pay with her death for what she had just done—that she saw clearly that it was all up with her and that she could not survive such an occurrence. I told her that I would forgive her and forget all about what she had done, but that I was determined to go away in the morning, since they wanted to get rid of me, and I made the lady promise that she would not poison herself. I remained in the room until six o'clock in the morning with the lady, whom I compelled to go back to bed, I remaining on a sofa beside the bed near her.'

After this scene, Briancourt at once set about procuring pistols, deeming them necessary to his safety; then he went to ask the advice of Monsieur Bocager, a professor of the law school, who had introduced him to Madame de Brinvilliers.

From the first day he saw the terrible marchioness, Briancourt had advanced from surprise to surprise; but his greatest astonishment awaited him in the study of the law professor. The young man said to him, 'Sir, I have a great secret to communicate to you; I think that you will give me good advice, and that you will tell the first president, whom you often see, what is going on, so that he may take the proper steps.' The professor's discomposure was evident in his features, and he leaned back uncomfortably in his chair. 'Monsieur Bocager turned very pale, and said nothing, except that I must keep my secret and not speak about it to the curé of St. Paul or any one else. He assured me that he would see to everything, and that I ought not to leave the Brinvilliers' house so soon, but wait some time, while he sought some new employment for me.' Briancourt asked himself whether all that he heard and saw were real events in a real world. How far had this terrible woman been to seek her accomplices? How far had she pushed her crimes?

'Two days afterwards,' continues Briancourt, 'the marquise told me that Monsieur Bocager was not so upright a man as I imagined, as I should see some day. And as I was passing down the street in the evening, just opposite St. Paul's, two pistol-shots were fired at me, without my being able to tell whence they came, and one of them pierced my coat. Seeing that I was marked down, I went next day to Sainte-Croix' house, carrying two pistols, having left a man at the street door to see that it remained open. I told Sainte-Croix that he was a villain and a scoundrel, that he would be broken on the wheel, and that he had caused the death of several people of quality. He declared that he had never caused anybody's death, but that if I would go behind the Hôpital Général with pistols he would give me every kind of satisfaction; to which I replied that I was not a soldier, but that if I were attacked I should defend myself.'

Such was the strange existence of the poor bachelor in theology, tutor to the children of the Marquis de Brinvilliers. In his fear of poison he was continually swallowing some nostrum or other by way of antidote.

The marquis himself lived in equal terror. He knew what was going on, and took things philosophically. Here is a sketch of a dinner at his house. 'The marchioness put Sainte-Croix on her right; the marquis was at the sideboard end of the table. The latter was very carefully served by a domestic specially attached to his person, to whom he always said: "Don't change my glass, but rinse it every time you give me anything to drink."' When the evening was over, the marquis retired to his room; Sainte-Croix and the marchioness went to the lady's room, and Briancourt went upstairs with the children. With the horrors of crime there were thus mingled scenes of burlesque.

Accommodating as her husband was, the marchioness began to poison him; then, struck with remorse, she called in to attend him one of the most famous physicians of the time, Dr. Brayer.

'She wished to marry Sainte-Croix,' writes Madame de Sévigné, 'and with that intention often gave her husband poison. Sainte-Croix, not anxious to have so evil a woman as his wife, gave counter-poisons to the poor husband, with the result that, shuttlecocked about like this five or six times, now poisoned, now unpoisoned, he still remained alive.' Brinvilliers emerged from this violent treatment with a weakness in the legs. Afterwards he always carried theriac about with him, that being regarded as an antidote; he took it from time to time, and gave doses to his people.

Briancourt, however, succeeded in escaping from the service of his formidable mistress, and, under the baleful impression of what he had seen in the world, he retired to Aubervilliers, where he lived in solitude, giving lessons in the establishment of the Fathers of the Oratory there. Seven or eight months had passed when the marchioness came to see him; then she sent from time to time to ask how he was doing. It was at Aubervilliers that one evening, on July 31, 1672, he received from his late mistress a very urgent note, begging him to go immediately to Picpus, where she had an important communication to make to him. There had just happened an event which was to entail incalculable consequences: on July 30 Sainte-Croix died in his mysterious dwelling in the cul-de-sac of the Place Maubert.

A widespread legend makes Sainte-Croix' death the result of a chemical experiment; it is said that the glass mask with which he covered his face to protect it from the poisonous vapours had broken. But he really died a natural death after an illness of some months, in the course of which he was visited by several persons who have left their testimony in regard to the matter. In the legendary laboratory of the cul-de-sac there was found indeed a furnace of 'digestion.' Sainte-Croix 'philosophised' there, that is, worked at the philosopher's stone, and more particularly at solidifying mercury, that eternal dream of the alchemists.

Madame de Brinvilliers soon learned of the death of her lover. Her first cry was, 'The little box!'

II. HER TRIAL

Sainte-Croix died overwhelmed in debt. His things were all put under seal. The seals were raised on August 8, 1672, by Commissary Picard, assisted by a sergeant named Creuillebois, two notaries, the agent of the widow, and an agent of the creditors. The three first meetings had passed without incident when a Carmelite monk who was present handed to the commissary the key of the private room in which the furnace was kept. Entering, they saw on the table a rolled-up paper bearing the words, 'My confession.' The persons present decided without hesitation to keep the paper secret, and to burn it on the spot. They found, further, at the end of a shelf, a small box, oblong in shape and red in colour, from which hung a key. It contained some phials, some of which were filled with a clear liquid like water, others with a liquid of reddish colour; and in addition, there were the letters addressed by Madame de Brinvilliers to Sainte-Croix, the two promissory notes signed by the marchioness after the poisoning of her father and brothers, and a receipt and power of attorney relating to a sum of 10,000 livres lent by Pennautier, receiver-general of the clergy, to Monsieur and Madame de Brinvilliers through the agency of Sainte-Croix.

These two last papers were in a sealed envelope on which was written: 'Papers to be restored to the Sieur Pennautier, receiver-general of the clergy, as belonging to him; and I humbly beg those into whose hands they fall, to be good enough to return them to him at my death, they being of no consequence except to him alone.'

Sainte-Croix had addressed the little box, with its contents, to Madame de Brinvilliers in these terms: 'I humbly beg those into whose hands this box falls to do me the favour to return it into the hands of the Marquise de Brinvilliers, who lives in Rue Neuve-Saint-Paul, since all that it contains concerns her and belongs to her alone, and moreover it is of no use to anybody in the world but herself; and in case she dies before I do, to burn it, and all that is in it, without opening it or meddling with it; and so that no one may pretend ignorance, I swear by the God I adore, and all that is most holy, that I state nothing but the truth. If perchance any one contravenes my intentions, just and reasonable as they are, I charge it in this world and the next upon his conscience, for discharge of my own, and declare that this is my last will. Made at Paris, afternoon, May 25, 1670. *Signed*: Sainte-Croix.' Below were these words: 'There is a single packet addressed to Monsieur Pennautier, which is to be given to him.' The very energy of these formulæ impressed Commissary Picard. He sealed up the case and confided it to the care of two sergeants, Cluet and Creuillebois, so that the inventory might be made by the civil lieutenant in person. Sergeant Creuillebois took the box home.

It was Sainte-Croix' widow who on August 8—that is, the day when the box was discovered—sent word to Madame de Brinvilliers at Picpus that things belonging to her were under seal. The marchioness instantly sent some one to find the box. As that was no longer in Sainte-Croix' house, a servant was sent off to Commissary Picard to tell him that Madame de Brinvilliers desired to speak to him without delay. Picard answered that he was busy. The marchioness, however, herself hurried to Madame de Sainte-Croix, insisting on the box being given to her. It was nine o'clock at night. 'She complained of its having been sealed up, offered money to obtain it, proposed to break the seals in order to take out what was inside, and to substitute something else.' But the box had been taken away. 'It's very amusing,' she said, 'for Commissary Picard to carry off a box that belongs to me!' She got some one to take her to Sergeant Cluet, whom she made come down, so that she might speak to him from her carriage. 'The lady told him that Pennautier had come to her, and told her that he was anxious about the box, and would give fifty golden louis to have what was in it. She also said that all that was in the said box concerned Pennautier and herself, and that they had done everything in concert.' We see here the first step in a manœuvre which Madame de Brinvilliers afterwards developed. Knowing that several of the papers in the box concerned Pennautier, she sought to link her cause with the financier's, speculating on his high position and influence.

Cluet answered that he could do nothing without the commissary. Accordingly the marchioness hurried off to him at eleven o'clock at night. Picard sent down word that he could not receive her till the morning.

In the morning, August 9, the commissary received a visitor from a Châtelet[3] attorney named Delamarre, to whom the marchioness had intrusted her interests. He told the commissary that the little box was of great importance to Madame de Brinvilliers, begging him to send it back to her, and saying 'that she would give him all she had in the world.' 'There came also a man in black' (it was Briancourt) 'who told him that the marchioness would give him anything he could wish for.'

Madame de Brinvilliers understood that the box was not to be given up, and made preparations for flight. 'Delamarre, her attorney, repaired to Picpus at ten o'clock at night and carried off her principal furniture, which was even thrown hastily out of the windows.' The marchioness, however, sent for Cluet and Creuillebois to come to Picpus. She changed the line of her defence, and told Creuillebois that 'Sainte-Croix was clever enough to have forged the letters, but that she would find a way out, and had good friends.' To Madame de Sainte-Croix, who also went to Picpus, she said that she had nothing to do with the box, that it could only contain trifles, that she had not seen Sainte-Croix for a long time, that these were forged letters, and that she had a complete justification. She went on, in order to spread it abroad that her interests were connected with those of Pennautier: 'If it trickles on me, it will rain on Pennautier.' She said to the wife of a Châtelet clerk named Fausset, who spoke to her of the rumours of poisoning that were already going about. 'There is nothing in it: it will blow over; there is a man accused with me who will give four or six thousand livres to arrange matters,' adding that 'he was not of high rank, but was very rich.'

The seals placed on the box were raised by the civil lieutenant on August 11. Madame de Brinvilliers was represented by her attorney, who made the following declaration: 'That if there was found a promise signed by Lady Brinvilliers for the sum of 30,000 livres, it was a document obtained from her by fraud, against which, in case the signature proved genuine, she intended to appeal, in order to have it declared null and void.'

The liquids and the powder contained in the chest were tested on animals, death being the result. Experts decided that they contained poison, but could not determine its nature. The general belief was that it was arsenic.

Madame de Brinvilliers and Pennautier were soon the engrossing topic of conversation in Paris. Fantastic rumours circulated about the poisons found in the box, of which Madame de Sévigné made herself the sedulous echo.

The marchioness hastened to pay a visit to Pennautier. He was not at home. His wife turned her out neck and crop. Pennautier responded by taking a step which did him honour: he went to Picpus to see Madame de Brinvilliers. Asked later, after his arrest, what was his motive in going to Picpus, he replied that, not believing Madame de Brinvilliers guilty of such a crime, he went to pay her his respects, as is usual on such occasions. Speaking of this step of his, his enemies wrote: 'Actuated by a sentiment of courtesy, he neglected his most obvious interests, in which life, honour, and fortune were at stake; his excessive politeness made him forgetful of all his interests. What a rare and marvellous character! How free from thoughts of self!' These lines, written with ironical intention, really express the truth. Not long before, Monsieur and Madame de Brinvilliers had done Pennautier a great service in a moment of difficulty by the loan of 30,000 livres; and he seized the opportunity to show that he had not forgotten their kindness.

P. L. Reich de Pennautier—Pennautier was the name of an estate in the neighbourhood of Carcassonne—though scarcely thirty-five years old, had already made an enormous fortune. His two appointments as receiver-general for the clergy and treasurer of the Languedoc Exchange brought him in hundreds of thousands of francs annually. He was one of the most active and intelligent of Colbert's lieutenants. On such questions as the resuscitation of the French manufacture of fine cloth, the Languedoc canal, the purchase of Greek MSS. in the Levant, the draining of the fens of Aigues-Mortes, the name of Pennautier is linked with that of Colbert in enterprises of the utmost utility 'From a petty cashier,' says Saint-Simon, 'Pennautier became treasurer of the clergy and treasurer of the States of Languedoc, and enormously rich. He was a tall and well-made man, with a gallant and dignified air, courteous and eminently obliging; he had plenty of intelligence, and had many connections in society.

On August 22 the civil lieutenant summoned Madame de Brinvilliers and Pennautier to appear at the examination of the documents found in the box. Pennautier was in the country; the marchioness was represented by her attorney, who repeated his protests. A third personage appeared on the scene, namely, La Chaussée. He fancied his audacity would save him, and from the first had opposed the sealing of the house, on the ground that he had deposited with the deceased, in whose service he had been for seven years, 200 pistoles and 100 silver crowns which should be, he said, behind the window of the study in a bag, with a note proving that the money belonged to him. He claimed also a number of papers, which he described. The knowledge that La Chaussée displayed of Sainte-Croix' laboratory awakened suspicion. When Commissary Picard told the whilom valet that the confiscated box had just been opened, he stood petrified with confusion for a moment, then fled precipitately, leaving the commissary in open-eyed amazement. The same day he left Gaussin, a bath-proprietor whose service he had entered, and, concealing himself during the day, roamed about Paris at night-time till he was arrested on September 4 at six o'clock in the morning by a police officer named Thomas Regnier. La Chaussée was very crestfallen as he walked down the street.

From that moment the gravest suspicions were entertained against Madame de Brinvilliers, but there was a reluctance to arrest her because of her rank. Regnier repaired to Picpus and told her bluntly that he had found La Chaussée, and that he had learned a good many things from the commissary. The marchioness blushed. 'What is it, madam? You say nothing?' But the lady, changing the subject, asked him to escort her to mass. When they returned, she spoke to him again about the box. She seemed a prey to uneasiness. 'But madam,' said Regnier, 'surely you are not mixed up in this business?' 'Why should I be?' she replied. 'That villain La Chaussée, when with Commissary Picard, must have said something against you, and would say it again if he was captured.' 'It would be well to take the villain to Picardy,' said the marchioness. She said also that she had long been pressing Sainte-Croix to return the box, and that Pennautier was involved with herself in the matter. Regnier left Madame de Brinvilliers and went to find Briancourt at Vertus. He told him, to begin with, that he had arrested La Chaussée, and Briancourt exclaimed, 'Then she is a lost woman!' He went on to speak of the poison which she had often talked about, and said that she had several sorts of it in her house.

Meanwhile Madame Antoine d'Aubray, widow of the last civil lieutenant and sister-in-law of the marchioness, had learned what was going on—that her husband had actually died of poison as the doctors had suspected. Hastening to Paris, she presented a petition to the Châtelet on September 10, and was admitted a plaintiff in a civil action for damages against La Chaussée and Madame de Brinvilliers. The latter had just fled to England, with no other attendant than a kitchenmaid. All suspicions were at once confirmed. The action against La Chaussée heard before the Châtelet ended on February 23, 1673, in a decree sentencing the defendant to the preliminary torture, *manentibus indiciis*. If the wretched man gave proof of endurance under torture, it would be the salvation both of himself and of the marchioness. Madame d'Aubray made a passionate intervention. She appealed to the Parlement,[4] endeavouring to prove, in a fresh affidavit, that the charges had been fully sustained, and that it was not permissible to have recourse to a preliminary dubious in itself and one that might snatch the criminals from due punishment. The case was reopened at the Tournelle.[5] In spite of a skilful defence, La Chaussée was condemned to death on March 24, 1673. The sentence set forth that he was convicted of poisoning, and condemned to be broken alive on the wheel after being put to the 'question ordinary and extraordinary,' and that Madame de Brinvilliers was to be beheaded for contempt of court.

When submitted to torture, La Chaussée displayed uncommon courage and denied everything. The mode of torture adopted was that of the boot. The legs of the condemned man were placed between boards, which were driven by degrees closer together by the introduction of eight wedges in succession, the legs being thus horribly mangled. Released from the machine, he was carried on a mattress to a corner of the fireplace, and refreshed with brandy. In anticipation of instant death, La Chaussée voluntarily confessed his crimes, including the poisoning of Villequoy's tart, and then spoke of the iniquities of Madame de Brinvilliers. 'What accuser,' says La Reynie, 'would have been listened to for a moment if God had not permitted the capture of this valet, whom the first judges could not condemn for want of proof, but whom the Parlement condemned on conjectures and strong presumptions; and if God had not touched the heart of this wretch, who, after having suffered torture in absolute silence, confessed his crimes a moment before being executed?' La Chaussée was broken on the wheel the same day.

Taking refuge in London, the marchioness led a wretched existence, in distress which she found insupportable, and a prey to incessant fears.

Louis XIV had from the first taken a very strong personal interest in this case. It was his sincere desire that the investigation should be made as complete and luminous as possible, and he was determined to follow up and strike at all the accomplices, however high they were placed. The Secretaries of State had not awaited the declarations made by La Chaussée on May 24, 1673, before requesting the English Government to extradite the accused woman. In November and December 1672 several letters were exchanged between Colbert and his brother the Marquis de Croissy, then French ambassador at the court of Charles II. The king of England consented to the extradition, but declared that he could not allow the arrest to be made by English officers; that would have to be undertaken by France. Croissy was highly embarrassed. The embassy was not provided with tools for such jobs. Colbert insisted, and at length the ambassador was on the point of winning Charles's consent to the employment of English police, when Madame de Brinvilliers, taking fright, quitted England for the Netherlands.

Meanwhile her husband, this amazing Marquis de Brinvilliers, had quietly taken up his abode, with his children and domestics, in the chateau of Offémont, belonging to the estate of his father-in-law and two brothers-in-law whom his wife had poisoned. He had taken possession of the surrounding domain, and actually it was not till two *lettres de cachet* had been signed by Louis XIV, bearing date February 22 and March 31, 1674, ordering him to leave the chateau and never approach within three leagues of it, that he decided to allow the widow of the civil lieutenant to enter upon the enjoyment of her own property.

We have very little information on the life of the marchioness between her departure from London and her arrest on March 25, 1676, at Liége in a convent where she had taken shelter. She had gone from London to the Netherlands, then into Picardy, the country conquered by King Louis, thence to Cambrai and Valenciennes, where she entered a convent, but was obliged to leave it on account of the war. From Valenciennes she fled to Antwerp, then to Liége. She had nothing to support her but an annuity of 500 livres, which fell to 250 on the death of her sister; she was sometimes 'reduced to borrowing a crown.' While at Cambrai, she appears to have sent asking her husband to join her there; his answer was, 'She would poison me like the rest.'

It came to the ears of Louvois that Madame de Brinvilliers was in hiding at Liége. He at once despatched Desgrez, the captain of police, a man of tried ability. Desgrez was instructed to make all speed, for the French troops then in possession of Liége were on the point of handing over the town to the Spaniards. Michelet and the majority of historians have woven the arrest of the marchioness into a romance. Desgrez, a handsome fellow, disguises himself as a courtly abbé, and wins a warm welcome from the lady, always eager for gallant adventures: at the rendezvous, the lover appears as a police officer, accompanied by a number of archers. As a matter of fact, the arrest was managed in the simplest manner, 'on the last day,' writes La Reynie, 'that the king's authority was recognised in the town of Liége.' It was not even Desgrez who carried it through, but a French political agent in the Netherlands, a former clerk of Fouquet's named Bruant, otherwise Descarrières. 'The burgomasters,' wrote the latter to Louvois on March 25, 'have behaved so well that they confided to me their master-key to go and arrest this lady, without wanting to know why it was to be done.' Next day, March 26, Descarrières wrote again to Louvois: 'I arranged that the detective (Desgrez) should be present as privy to the capture'; he informed him also that a small box was seized on the lady's person, at which 'she appeared much agitated, and at first told mayor Goffin that her confession was in the casket,' begging him to have it restored to her. Descarrières sealed the box with his own seal and that of Desgrez.

La Reynie says upon this subject: 'It was God who ordained that this wretched woman, who fled from kingdom to kingdom, should be careful to write and carry with her the proofs necessary to her condemnation.' This confession, in which the marchioness recalls in a few pages all the crimes of her life, was published by Armand Fouquier; but its flavour is so strong that the editor was not able to reproduce the original text, but had to translate the principal passages into Latin.

From Liége the marchioness was led under guard to Maestricht, where she arrived on March 29; she was there locked up, and rigorously watched in the town hall. Immediately after her arrest, the prisoner tried to commit suicide by swallowing the fragments of a glass which she had broken between her teeth. She swallowed pins, too, but did not succeed in killing herself. Resne, one of the sentries, vigorously abused her: 'You are a wicked woman! After having dyed your hands in the blood of your family, you want to do away with yourself!' She answered, 'If I did so, it was under evil counsel.' On another occasion Desgrez was informed that the lady had endeavoured to commit suicide in a far more horrible fashion. 'Ah, you wretch!' he cried. 'I see that you want to do for yourself, and that you did poison your brothers!' She replied: 'If I had only had good advice! We often have our evil moments.' The archers who guarded her during her journey from Liége to Paris gave the judges a description of this third attempt at suicide which it is impossible to reproduce. The following is a note from Emmanuel de Coulanges, forwarded by Madame de Sévigné to Madame de Grignan: 'She stuck a stick into herself; guess where: it was not in her eye, nor her mouth, nor her ear, nor her nose, nor was she absolutely brutal.'

During the journey Madame de Brinvilliers was escorted by the Marshal d'Estrades in person as far as Huy, and from Huy to Rocroi by the troops of Monsieur de Montal. The prisoner's character displayed itself in all its untamed energy. Locked up at Maestricht, she suggested to Antoine Barbier, an archer of the guard who had won her confidence, to make a gag and a rope-ladder: the gag was for Desgrez and the rope-ladder for her own escape. She promised Barbier a thousand pistoles. At other times she urged him to help her throttle Desgrez, kill the *valet de chambre*, detach the two leading horses from the coach, take the documents, the casket with her confession, and another important paper, and burn them all, for which purpose he was to carry a lighted match.

She wrote to former servants who remained faithful to her, and actually succeeded in getting letters delivered to them, for they endeavoured to rescue her, and tried to bribe her guardians.

She persisted in the plan she had devised in regard to the accusation under which Pennautier lay. She asked Barbier for ink to write to him; he gave her some, and feigned to have despatched the letter. And when he asked her if Pennautier was one of her friends, 'Yes, yes,' she replied, 'and he is as much interested in my safety as I am myself.' Another time she said: 'He must be much more frightened than I am. I have been questioned about him, but I have said nothing, and have too much feeling to charge him: half of the aristocracy are involved too, and I should ruin them all if I spoke.' This she repeated several times.

At Mézières the marchioness met Denis de Palluau, a Parlement counsellor, whom the court had deputed to put her through a first interrogation. Corbinelli, the friend of Madame de Sévigné, wrote to Madame de Grignan: 'The king has required the Parlement to depute Palluau, counsellor in the High Court, to go to Rocroi, where he is to interrogate the Brinvilliers, because they don't wish to wait till she arrives here, where the whole bar is connected with the poor criminal.'

The first examination to which Palluau subjected the marchioness is dated Mézières, April 17, 1676. The prisoner took refuge in systematic denials.

'Questioned on the first article of her confession, as to the house she set on fire, she said she had not done so, and that when she had written such things she was out of her mind.

'Questioned on the six remaining articles of her confession, she said she did not know what that was, and remembered nothing about it.

'Asked if she had not poisoned her father and brothers, she said she knew nothing about it.

'Asked if it was not La Chaussée who had poisoned her brothers, she said she knew nothing of all that.

'Eight letters were shown her, and she was enjoined to disclose to whom she had written them; she said she did not remember.

'Asked why she wrote to Théria to secure the box, she said she did not know what that was.

'Asked why, in writing to Théria, she said she was lost if he did not get the box and win his case, she said she did not remember.'

The marchioness was lodged in the Conciergerie on the day of her arrival in Paris, namely, April 26. She was left under the guard of the archer Barbier, to whom she continued to intrust letters, which he said he carried to their addresses, but which he really handed to the judges.

On April 29 she wrote to Pennautier:—

'I hear from my friend that you are intending to help me in this business, and you may be sure that this will be to me an additional obligation to all your kindnesses. Wherefore, sir, if you really mean this, you must please not lose any time, and not be seen with the people who will go to find out from you in what way you wish to manage things. I think it would be much to the purpose if you did not show yourself too much, but your friends must know where you are, for the counsellor severely examined me about you at Mézières.'

There follows a recommendation to buy the silence of the 'Bernardins widow,' that is, the widow of Sainte-Croix, who lodged in the Rue des Bernardins.

Madame de Brinvilliers disclosed by and by the motives of her conduct in regard to Pennautier. 'I do not know at all,' she said on the night before her death, 'that Monsieur Pennautier ever had any communication with Sainte-Croix about the poisons, and I could not accuse him without betraying my conscience. But as a note concerning him was found in the box, and as I saw him many times with Sainte-Croix, I thought that their friendship had progressed so far as to have dealings in poisons, and in this suspicion I ventured to write to him as though I knew it was so, running no risk of injuring my own case thereby, and inwardly arguing thus: if there was any connection between them in regard to the poisons, Monsieur Pennautier will believe that I must know the secret, considering the step I am taking, and that will induce him to exert himself on my behalf as much as on his own, for fear lest I accuse him; and if he is innocent, my letter is waste labour. I risk nothing but the indignation of a person who would be careful not to stand up for me, nor to render me any service if I had written him nothing.'

The letters of the prisoner increased the suspicions against Pennautier to such an extent that a decree was issued for the arrest of the unlucky functionary, and he was shut up in the Conciergerie in the same room that Ravaillac[6] had occupied.

Marie Vosser, widow of Hannyvel de Saint-Laurent, Pennautier's predecessor in the office of receiver for the clergy, was striving to arouse public opinion against Pennautier. She accused him of having poisoned her husband on May 2, 1669, in order to succeed him in an office of considerable emolument. She overwhelmed him with affidavits drawn up by Vautier, one of the best advocates in Paris. These damaging documents were in everybody's hands.

The rapidly acquired wealth of Pennautier, far from protecting him in the opinion of the public, had raised up a thousand enemies who diligently spread false reports about him. The people regarded his influence and wealth with amazement, the nobility with envy. On the other hand, Pennautier, like Fouquet, found some faithful friends, a circumstance which does honour to the time. 'It is wonderful,' says Saint-Simon, 'how many of the most notable men are working on his behalf.' This generosity of sentiment was the more admirable in that the recollection of the disgrace which overwhelmed Fouquet's friends was present to every mind. The Cardinal de Bonsy, the Duke de Verneuil, the Archbishop of Paris, Harlay de Champvallon, and Colbert were among the most active. The judges, who were suspected by Louis XIV himself of having been corrupted, gave proof of an admirable independence.

Pennautier was writing a letter to one of his cousins in his office on June 15, 1676, when the police made a sudden raid upon his room. What he had written was as follows:—'I think that, for our friend, a stay of a month in the country will suffice....' Startled by this sudden interruption, Pennautier nervously put this note in his mouth as though to swallow it. This fact remained in the sequel the sole charge which the prosecutor could bring against him, after Madame de Brinvilliers had entirely exculpated him. His declarations under examination were of convincing frankness; moreover, in a statement printed in answer to the pamphlets of Sainte-Croix' widow, he established incontestably the falsity of some points on which his adversaries were endeavouring to base their accusations. These latter found themselves reduced to maintaining that the official reports drawn up at the time when the seals had been broken at Sainte-Croix' place had been falsified.

'I am accused of having poisoned Saint-Laurent,' added Pennautier; 'but has it been so much as proved that he died of poison? It is at least singular to declare me guilty of a crime that was never committed, for the reports of the doctors, as well as the circumstances under which he died, prove that his death was natural.'

The close of Pennautier's reply was crushing for his accuser. He pointed out that Madame de Saint-Laurent had waited six years before bringing her case into court. How was that silence explained? Saint-Laurent being dead, Pennautier was appointed to his office of receiver-general for the clergy. 'Saint-Laurent's wife gave him her nomination on June 12, 1669; the same day they drew up a sort of contract together, by which the lady reserved half the emoluments of the office, and Pennautier gave 2000 pistoles to the Sieur de Mannevillette, who claimed from the lady the right to return to this office, in accordance with the deed of defeasance given him by Saint-Laurent when the Sieur de Mannevillette resigned that office in his favour on March 17, 1669. The dame de Saint-Laurent quietly enjoyed this moiety of the emoluments of the office until the last day of December 1675, when the agreement terminated; and if Pennautier had been willing to renew the agreement with her, when the general assembly of the clergy did him the honour to elect him receiver-general for ten years, which will end on the last day of December 1685, those who know the dame de Saint-Laurent are convinced that she would never have accused Pennautier of poisoning the Sieur de Saint-Laurent her husband.'

We have dwelt at some length on this incident because of the important part played by Pennautier in the restoration of commerce and industry in France under the direction of Colbert.

Nothing was talked about in Paris but Madame de Brinvilliers and Pennautier—'a grave injustice to the war,' as Madame de Sévigné said.

Through the privilege of nobility, Madame de Brinvilliers was brought before the highest judicial tribunal in the kingdom—the High Court and the Tournelle in conjunction. She requested a counsel to assist her in her defence, but the request was refused, at least provisionally.

The court was presided over by the first president, Lamoignon. Between April 29 and July 16, 1676, the case occupied twenty-two sittings. The marchioness displayed an energy and force of will which was a constant subject of astonishment to her judges. She denied everything obstinately, and contradicted her accusers in a hard and haughty voice, but never failed in the respect due to the judges—a respect in which pride and nobility mingled, and which made the audience feel that she considered herself at least the equal of the men judging her.

When they came to read the account of the examination at Mézières on April 17, there occurred a scene which was not unexpected. The following is an extract from the official report of the proceedings:—

'At the reading of these interrogatories, the first president wished to intervene and postpone it until after the confession had been read. This raised a difficulty, and a discussion ensued as to whether it was allowable to question the lady on these particular crimes, such as sodomy and incest, which being on this occasion only a matter of confession, it seemed that they should be kept a great secret; some were for, others against.

'Monsieur de Palluau said that, having consulted the law-doctors, he had been told that, a confession having been found *en route*, it ought to have been burnt under penalty, as some believed, of mortal sin.

'Other doctors held that the said Palluau, in his capacity as judge, had had no choice but to give a description of the confession, and to interrogate her on the aforesaid paper beginning, *I accuse myself, my father,* etc.

'The first president held that the question was extremely uncertain, yet he thought the papers ought to be read.

'The President de Mesmes held that this sort of confession had been utilised in Christian countries, and quoted the epistle of St. Leo, showing that the judges had made use of them.

'Nivelle, advocate, urged the contrary opinion.

'The first president answered that the epistle of St. Leo was utterly opposed to the contention of Monsieur de Mesmes, and that there was nothing for it but to resume the reading.

'The question having been argued, the reading was continued.

'Asked if she had not made her confession, and to whom she ought to confess, she answered that she had had no intention whatever of making a confession, and knew no priests or monks to whom she ought to confess.

'Monsieur Roujault reported in the afternoon that he had put the question to Monsieur Benjamin, an ecclesiastical judge, to Monsieur du Saussoy and other casuists, and to Monsieur de Lestocq, doctor and professor in theology, who all agreed that this paper should be seen, and Madame de Brinvilliers questioned on it; that the secrecy of the confessional could only be between the confessor and the penitent, and a paper having been found purporting to be a confession, it might be read by the judges.'

On July 13, 1676, a terrible deposition was heard—that of Briancourt, who related in detail his mistress's life. He spoke in a voice broken by emotion. The marchioness contradicted him with the same cold, haughty impassivity. 'Her spirit quite overawes us,' said President Lamoignon. 'We worked yesterday at her case till eight o'clock in the evening; she was confronted with Briancourt for thirteen hours, and to-day another five, and she has gone through both ordeals with surprising courage. No one could have more respect for the judges, nor more scorn for the witness confronting her: she taunted him with being a besotted lackey, bundled out of the house for his disorderly conduct, and one whose testimony should not be received against her.' But she was lost. The marchioness saw looming before her the spectacle of her ignominious punishment—the public penance on her knees before the porch of Notre Dame, clad only in her shift, torch in hand; she saw the instruments of torture, the thought of which might make the boldest shudder, then the scaffold, the stake, the 'tomb of fire' whence the hand of the executioner would scatter her ashes, under the gaze of the mob. The judges themselves, who were about to condemn her, felt a tightening at the heart. And when Briancourt, at the close of his deposition, his eyes streaming with tears, his voice choked with sobs, said: 'I warned you many a time, madam, about your disorders and your cruelty, and that your crimes would ruin you,' the marchioness replied—a wonderful reply in its pride and self-control—'You are chicken-hearted, you are crying!' Could one find such a saying in Roman history, or in Corneille? We prefer the bare cold version of the official minute to the version reported by President Lamoignon to the abbé Pirot: 'She insulted Briancourt about the tears he shed at the remembrance of the death of her brothers, when he declared that she had made him her confidant in regard to their poisoning, and told him that he was a villain to weep before all these gentlemen—that it resulted from a mean spirit. All this was said with great coolness, and without any appearance of changing countenance during the five hours we all watched her to-day.'

Advocate Nivelle, on whom fell the heavy task of presenting the defence of the accused lady, acquitted himself of it with remarkable success. His defence was still renowned in the eighteenth century. It was broad in style, and some of his phrases were of great beauty.

'The enormity of the crimes,' he said, 'and the rank of the person accused require proofs of the most convincing clearness, written, so to speak, with rays of sunlight.' He went on to ask if the proofs adduced against Madame de Brinvilliers were of this quality. He succeeded in throwing doubt on the sincerity of several of the more weighty depositions—that of Sergeant Cluet, for instance, who was devoted body and soul, he said, to the opposite party; to the widow d'Aubray, who sustained her part of plaintiff with the extremest animosity. The deposition of Edme Briscien, he maintained, should be entirely rejected, for the witness was not confronted with the marchioness, and on that point the rules of procedure were absolute. He very cleverly took advantage of some inconsistencies in La Chaussée's declaration after torture. The argument based on Sainte-Croix' famous box seemed to him to have as little weight. Indeed, the note of May 25, 1670, in which Sainte-Croix declared that the contents of the box belonged to the marchioness, was undoubtedly anterior to the introduction of poison bottles into the box; it applied only to the lady's letters to Sainte-Croix, in which there was no question of poison. Coming at last to the written confession seized at Liége, Nivelle strongly protested against the inferential proof of guilt which the judges drew from it. 'The last proof,' he said, 'relates to a paper found among those of the marchioness, in which she had written a religious confession. It is astounding that the accusers desired the judges to read this paper, for it was of a nature which laws human and divine hold sacred and inviolable under the seal of secrecy and silence demanded by the rules of one of the most august of mysteries, as I will prove by invincible arguments.' These arguments were exhausted in a minute study of the writings of the Church fathers and of ecclesiastical history, from which the advocate produced numerous examples and excerpts likely to imbue the judges with the profoundest respect for the secrecy of confession, under whatever form it might present itself.

Finally, Nivelle set himself to win a little sympathy, or at any rate pity, for his client. He depicted this woman as a frail thing, of noble birth, beautiful and sensitive by nature, a butt for several months past to calumnies prompted by hate, to the rough treatment and insults of archers, drunken soldiers, and coarse jailors; she had also been deprived of spiritual consolation, and even on Whitsunday had been refused permission to hear mass. Undoubtedly Nivelle largely contributed to that revulsion of feeling in favour of the marchioness which was so strongly marked during the last days.

The advocate concluded his address with a powerful appeal to the prosecutrix: 'The accuser ought not to press hardly against the lady, because she has already received satisfaction for the death of her husband in the exemplary punishment of that wretched criminal (La Chaussée) who slew him; she should rather wish that the family to which she is allied should not be sullied with an eternal disgrace, and that she should not incur the reproach of being wanting in natural feeling for her nephews, whom she ought to consider as her own children. The death of the late Messieurs d'Aubray has been publicly avenged, and if they could now tell us what they feel, they would doubtless show that the affection they always bore to their sister was a sign that they recognised how incapable she was of so unnatural a crime; they would themselves plead for their own blood, and be far indeed from sacrificing their relatives and exposing them to infamous punishment; they would prove that their highest satisfaction is to preserve their honour in preserving her life, and that otherwise it would be to punish themselves rather than to avenge them. But if they find their consolation in the acquittal of Lady Brinvilliers; if her children—who would suffer punishment as if they were guilty, and to whom life would become a torture and death a consolation—find in it the preservation of the honour of a family so notable as that from which their mother is sprung—these wise magistrates who are to judge her will also have more glory in giving to the public a famous example of their justice, their piety, and their sovereign equity, by declaring her innocent.'

On July 15, 1676, Madame de Brinvilliers appeared for the last time before her judges for her final cross-examination, and in the course of this long ordeal, in which for three hours her whole life was remorselessly dissected, she did not flag for a moment. She denied everything; she did not know what poison and antidote meant; her pretended confession was sheer madness. 'She did not appear affected by what the first president said, though, after he had done his part as judge, he assumed the tone of a merciful friend, and addressed to her words most admirably calculated to move her, and bring her to feel in some degree the lamentable state in which she was. The first president,' we read in a summary report of the trial, 'dwelt upon the dreadful illness of her father, on the perilous state she was in, and told her that she was engaged in perhaps the last act of her life; he invited her seriously to reflect on her evil conduct, which had drawn upon her the reproaches of her family, and even of those who had lived in sin with her. The President de Novion reminded her that her brother the civil lieutenant had suspected other persons, and that this suspicion had embittered his last moments. The first president told her also' (and this is one of the most curious features of the trial for the study of the moral ideas of the period), 'that the greatest of all her crimes, horrible as they were, was, not the poisoning of her father and brothers, but her attempt to poison herself. She was kept for another half hour, but would say nothing, merely showing signs of a little distress at heart.'

'The first president wept bitterly,' writes the abbé Pirot, 'and all the judges shed tears.' She alone kept her head proudly erect, and preserved undimmed the stony clearness of her blue eyes.

Taine has given in one line a marvellous definition of the character of Racine's heroines and the art of the poet himself: 'We imagine the tears which never appear in their beautiful eyes.' The sequel of our story will indicate, even more than the preceding pages, that Madame de Brinvilliers in some points resembled some of Racine's heroines, and will help to show with what exactitude the incomparable poet reproduced the models presented him by the society of his time.

In closing this memorable scene on July 15, President Lamoignon told the prisoner that, out of charity and on the plea of her sister the Carmelite nun, a person of the greatest merit and the highest virtue was being sent to her to console her and to exhort her to think of her soul's salvation. We are about to see coming upon the stage one of the most interesting figures in the drama, the sympathetic abbé, Edme Pirot.

III. HER DEATH

Edme Pirot was a professor of theology at the Sorbonne. Born at Auxerre on August 12, 1631, he was of the same age as the Marchioness of Brinvilliers. His discussions with Leibnitz had made his name famous throughout Europe. His was an ardent and sensitive soul: his heart was torn when he came in contact with the griefs of others. 'The delicacy of my temperament was so great,' he said, 'that I could never bear the sight of blood, not even my own, and at one time I had turned quite faint at the sight of a wound being dressed, and never since ventured to come within sight of a similar operation.' He had an acute and subtle intellect, endowed with a remarkable faculty for psychological insight.

President Lamoignon, in appointing the abbé Pirot to attend Madame de Brinvilliers, had given a fresh proof of his knowledge of men. He knew that the gentle and soul-stirring words of the priest would act on the heart of the prisoner, and perhaps obtain what all the machinery of justice had not succeeded in achieving—the revelation of her accomplices, the composition of her poisons and the proper antidotes to employ. 'It is for the public interest,' said Lamoignon to the abbé Pirot, 'that her crimes should die with her, and that she should acquaint us with all the consequences her poison might have, so far as she knows them; without which we should be unable to counteract them, and her poisons would survive her.' Further, it was his earnest desire to find in Pirot a priest whose exhortations would, at the hour of death, touch this rebellious soul and set it on the narrow road to salvation.

The good abbé has described the last day of Madame de Brinvilliers minute by minute. His story fills two volumes, one of the most extraordinary monuments literature can show. It is written with no regard for artistic effect: the conversations are reported at length, with repetitions and interminably wearisome details; but the clear, exact, and flowing style, the just and restrained expression of the keenest passions, continually remind us of the tragedies of Racine. *Phédre* and the abbé Pirot's story were composed in the same year; if the priest had given any thought to the public as he wrote, and had paid some attention to his style and to the avoidance of repetitions and prolixity, posterity unquestionably might well have signed both works with the same name.

Michelet has strikingly described the appearance of the priest in the tower of the Conciergerie:—

'Quaking with terror, Pirot was ushered into the Conciergerie, and taken to the top of the Montgommery tower; there he entered a room in which there were four persons—two warders, a wardress, and, farthest away from him, the monster.

'The monster was quite a little woman, dainty, with very soft blue eyes, marvellously beautiful. As soon as she saw Pirot, she prettily thanked a priest who up to then had attended her, and expressed with easy grace her absolute confidence in the learned abbé. He saw at once how much she was loved by those who lived with her. When she spoke of her death, the two men and the woman burst into tears. She seemed to love them too, and was kind and gentle with them, not proud at all; she made them eat at her table.

"'To be sure, sir,'" she said to Pirot, "'you are the priest that the first president has sent to console me; it is with you that I am to pass the little that remains of life: and I have long been impatient to see you.'"

"'I come, madam,'" answered Pirot, "'to render you in spiritual matters what service I can. I could wish it were in any other matter than this.'"

"'Sir,'" she rejoined, "'we must submit to everything.'"

And at that moment, turning towards an Oratorian named Father de Chevigny, she said: 'Father, I am obliged to you for bringing this gentleman, and for all the other visits you have been good enough to pay me; pray God for me, I beseech you: henceforth I shall speak to scarcely any one but the father here. I have matters to discuss with him that are spoken of in secret. Farewell.'

The Oratorian retired.

Madame de Brinvilliers seems to have been won at the outset by the affectionate expression of her confessor, and by his sincere and sympathetic words. Judgment had not yet been pronounced. 'My death is certain,' she said; 'I must not delude myself with hope. I have to tell you the story of all my life.' But the conversation drifted away to what was being said of her in society. 'I can imagine pretty well that they are talking a good deal about me, and that I have been for some time a byword among the people.' And her eyes flashed.

Pirot tried to show her that, assuming she was guilty, her duty was to disclose all her accomplices, to reveal the composition of her poisons and the means of counteracting them. She interrupted him: 'Sir, are there not some sins that are unpardonable in this world, either from their gravity or their number? Are there not some so atrocious or so numerous that the Church cannot remit them?' 'Believe, madam, that there are no sins irremissible in this life,' answered the priest, and he enlarged on this theme with force and warmth and an infectious faith. Conviction by degrees took possession of the prisoner's soul, and with it there dawned a gleam of regeneration, hope in a future life serene and happy—glorious, as the abbé said—and with the thought her heart was changed. "'Sir,'" she answered me, "I am convinced of all you tell me. I believe that God can pardon all sins; I believe that He has often exercised this power; but all my trouble now is to know whether He will apply His power to one so wretched as I." I told her that she must hope that God would take pity on her in His infinite mercy. She began to describe in general terms the whole of her life, and from that moment I saw that her heart was touched, and she burst into tears beholding her wretchedness.' By the contagion of his sympathetic kindness, and by the light of redemption, Pirot had in a few hours melted this heart of brass like wax.

'After she had given me an outline of her life, knowing that I had not yet said mass, she intimated spontaneously that it was time to say it, and that I might go down to the chapel for that purpose. She begged me say it to our Lady on her behalf, so as to obtain the pardon of which she stood in need, and asked me to come up again as soon as the sacrifice had been completed, saying that she would be present in spirit, since she was not permitted to attend in person, and that she thought of telling me in detail on my return that which she had so far told me only in general terms.

'After my mass,' continues Pirot, 'as I was taking a sip of wine in the jailer's room before returning to the tower, I learned from Monsieur de Sency, librarian to the Palais, that Madame de Brinvilliers was condemned. I went upstairs and found the marchioness awaiting me in great serenity.

'"It is only by dying by the hand of the executioner," she said, "that I can win salvation. If I had died at Liége before my arrest, where should I be now? And if I had not been taken, what would my end have been? I will confess my crime to the judges to whom I have denied it hitherto. I fancied I could conceal it, flattering myself that without my confession there would have been nothing to convict me, and that I was not bound to accuse myself. To-morrow, at my last examination, I mean to repair the ill that I have done at the others.

'"I beg you, sir," she went on suddenly, "to make my excuses to the first president. You will please see him on my behalf after my death, and will tell him that I ask his pardon, and that of all the judges, for the effrontery they have seen in me; that I believed it would serve my defence, and that I never believed there would be proof enough to condemn me without my avowal; that I now see things in a different light, and that I was touched yesterday by what he said to me, and that I put violent constraint on myself to prevent my features from showing what I felt. Ask him to forgive me for the offence I gave to the whole bench assembled to judge me, and to beg the other judges to pardon me."

'It was thus,' Pirot continues, 'that she went on relating to me the whole matter until half-past one, when a servant came and brought the cloth for dinner. She took nothing but two fresh eggs and a little soup, and talked to me, while I was eating, about indifferent things, with very great freedom of mind and a tranquillity which surprised me, as if she were entertaining me at dinner in a country house. She invited to the table the two men and the women who were her usual guard. "Sir," she said to me, after she had told them to sit down, "you will not mind our dispensing with ceremony for you? They are accustomed to eat with me to keep me company, and we shall do so to-day if you do not object. This," she said to them, "is the last meal I shall take with you." And turning towards the woman who was beside her, she said: "Madam, my poor Du Rus, you will soon be quit of me; I have long been a trouble to you, but it will soon be over. To-morrow you will be able to go to Dranet. You will have time enough for that. In seven or eight hours you will have me no longer to bother you, for I do not think you have the heart to see my end."

'She said all this with a coolness and serenity which indicated rather a natural equality of mind than an affected pride. And as these people from time to time burst into tears and withdrew to conceal them from her, she, noticing it, threw me a glance of pity, though she shed no tears, as though sorry for their grief, almost as a mother might do on her deathbed, when, seeing around her her weeping servants, she looks at the confessor kneeling near her and marks the sorrow their affection gives him.

'From time to time she urged me to eat, and scolded the jailer for putting cabbage in the soup. She asked me with much politeness to allow her to drink my health. I thought that I might do her some pleasure in drinking to hers, and it was not difficult to show her this little attention. She asked me to excuse her for not serving me, careful not to say that she had no knife for that purpose, so as not to give the slightest shadow of complaint.

'"Sir," she said to me at the end of the meal, "it is fast-day to-morrow, and though it will be a very tiring day for me"—she was to undergo torture and then be beheaded—"I have no intention of eating meat." "Madam," I replied, "if you need a meat soup to sustain you, there will be no occasion to stand on scruples; it will not be out of fastidiousness, but from pure necessity, and the law of the Church is not rigorous in such a case." "Sir," she replied, "I would not be particular if I needed it and you ordered it; but I am sure it will not be necessary. All I require is a little soup this evening at supper-time, and again at eleven o'clock; to-day they will make it a little stronger than usual, and with that, and a couple of eggs I can take at the torture, I shall get through to-morrow."

'It is true,' adds the good priest, 'that I was thunderstruck at all this composure, and I shivered when I heard her tell the jailer, so quietly, that the soup was to be stronger that evening than usual, and that two servings were to be kept for her before midnight.

'I saw in her at this moment much affection for Monsieur de Brinvilliers, and as it was generally believed that she had always had little enough love for him, I was surprised to find that she had so much. Indeed, it appeared to me to verge towards excess, and for half an hour I saw her more distressed for him than for herself.' And when Pirot, to test her, said that her husband appeared very insensible to her approaching fate, he drew from her a dignified reply: he must not judge things so hastily, she told him, or without intimate knowledge, and that up to that day she had only had to congratulate herself on her husband.

She asked for a pen, and with a rapid hand wrote this astonishing letter to the Marquis de Brinvilliers:—

'Being as I am on the point of going to give account of my soul to God, I want to assure you of my affection, which will endure to the last moment of my life. I ask your pardon for all that I have done that I ought not to have done. I die an honourable death, brought upon me by my enemies. I forgive them with all my heart, and beseech you to forgive them. I hope that you will also forgive me for the disgrace that may be reflected on you. But remember that we are here only for a time, and perhaps ere long you yourself will have to go and render to God an exact account of all your actions, even your idle words, as I am now preparing to do. Watch over our temporal affairs and our children: bring them up in the fear of the Lord, and yourself set them an example. On this consult Monsieur Marillac and Madame Cousté. Offer up for me as many prayers as you can, and be assured that I die yours devotedly,

D'AUBRAY.'

Pirot objected that what she said about her death and her enemies was not correct. 'How so, sir?' she said. 'Are not those who have driven me to death my enemies, and is it not a Christian sentiment to forgive them their rancour?'

Pirot's answer was as might be expected, but it was to her a revelation which plunged her into great astonishment.

Then the confession was resumed.

'King David was troubled at the sight of his sin,' said Pirot, 'his heart pined with grief at the remembrance of his crimes. His flesh was bruised, his bones were broken, his heart quailed, his face, his bread, and his bed were bathed in his tears, his voice became hoarse with the cries he uttered to heaven in imploring mercy. His groaning was like that of the turtle-dove that ceaseth not. That also is the picture of the Magdalene. She watered the feet of Christ with her tears and did not cease to kiss them. Her holy tears which are never spent, her sacred kisses which continue without interruption, are marks of the greatness and constancy of her contrition for her sins, and her love for God. All these words and a thousand others like them,' adds Pirot, 'caused her to weep bitterly.'

Twice after dinner the priest was interrupted by the procurator-general, who came to see in what condition the prisoner was, and if she was disposed to confess her crimes before the court, to name her accomplices, and reveal the nature of her poisons. The marchioness replied that she would tell everything, but not till the morrow; that till then she did not wish to be interrupted in her preparation for death; and she persisted in her resolution in spite of the entreaties of Pirot, who would rather the confession had been made at once.

She spoke of her children, displaying a tender affection for them. "'Sir,' she said to me, "I have not asked to see them; that would only have upset both them and me. I beseech you to be a mother to them.'" Pirot replied that it was the Virgin who would serve them as mother, and that the marchioness should pray to her to maintain them in purity and humility all their life long. From the first, Pirot had probed his fair prisoner's character to the bottom. 'Ah!' she said, interrupting him, 'those are grand virtues! Do you know that, humbled though I be by my hapless present state, yet I do not feel humble enough? I am still attached to this world's glory, and it is hard to bear the shame with which I am loaded.' And to the priest's remarks she replied: 'I tell myself all that when I reflect, but that does not prevent feelings of pride and glory sometimes passing through my mind, as they are natural to me.' And she added words that must have terrified the unhappy priest: 'At this present hour in which I speak to you, there are still moments when I cannot regret having known the man (Sainte-Croix) whose acquaintance has been so fatal to me, or hate his friendship which is so dire to me and has brought upon me so many misfortunes.'

Pirot supped that evening with the prisoner; then, when night had fallen, he withdrew, promising to return in the morning. He was in great agitation, and on reaching his apartment he had recourse to his breviary. 'The image of the lady I had seen all day so powerfully possessed me that I could hardly attend to what I was reading: it seemed to me that I was for nearly half an hour circling round *Domine, labia mea aperies*, returning always to where I had begun. At last, seeing that I must get on, I applied myself a little more diligently to my reading, so as to be less distracted by this idea. But in spite of all my close attention, I was quite three hours in reciting my office.'

He has described at length his sleeplessness, the thoughts that crowded upon his mind, the anguish which choked him: 'I got no sleep at all. Those who know the delicacy of my nature, how sensitive I am to the misery and pain I see in persons who are indifferent to me, will have no difficulty in realising the depth of my sorrow for a lady whom I had seen so afflicted, and who was so near to my heart by reason of the interest I was bound to take in the salvation of the soul intrusted to me.' Stretching out his clasped hands towards heaven, he cried: 'O God, I am greatly concerned for her whose salvation is as dear to me as my own; I die every moment for her, and all the reward I ask in the conflict I have to maintain with her before she closes her career is to see her crowned with Thee!'

In the morning Pirot returned to the prisoner. 'I was taken up the tower, where I found Father de Chevigny in tears as he closed a prayer with the lady, who greeted me with the same courage that I had seen in her on the previous evening.'

Madame de Brinvilliers has slept as peacefully as a child.

One of the first questions she put to her confessor related to a fear which had arisen in her mind, and the thought of which gave her much torture. 'Sir,' she said to me, 'you gave me yesterday some hope that I might be saved, but I cannot have the presumption to promise myself that that will be till after a long time in purgatory. How shall I know whether I am in purgatory or hell?' Pirot reassured her.

Soon afterwards a message came that Madame de Brinvilliers was to descend to hear her sentence read. 'She was prepared for death and torture; but she had not thought of the public penance or of the fire. She answered fearlessly, "In a moment, but just now we are finishing our conversation, this gentleman and I." We shortly finished our talk in great serenity.'

On leaving the prisoner, Pirot betook himself to the chapel of the Conciergerie. 'I said mass for her, and went into the jailer's room. I found him there, and he told me that he had accompanied her to the torture-chamber, and that after her sentence had been read, when the executioner approached to seize her, she looked him up and down without saying a word, and seeing a rope in his hand, she offered him her hands already clasped. I learned after dinner from the procurator-general that she had been agitated at the reading of her sentence, and that she got it read a second time.'

The sentence was dated July 16, 1676:—

'The court has declared and declares the said d'Aubray de Brinvilliers duly accused and convicted of having poisoned Maître Dreux d'Aubray her father, and the said d'Aubray, civil lieutenant and counsellor in the said court, her brothers, and for reparation has condemned and condemns the said d'Aubray de Brinvilliers to do public penance before the principal door of the church of Paris, where she will be taken in a cart, bare-footed, a rope on her neck, holding in her hands a lighted torch of two pounds weight, and there on her knees to say and declare that wickedly, from revenge and to have their property, she has poisoned her father and two brothers, and attempted the life of her late sister, of which she repents, and asks pardon of God, the king, and justice; this done, to be led and conducted in the said cart to the Place de Grève of this city, to have her head cut off there on a scaffold, which will be erected for that purpose on the said place; her body to be burned, and her ashes thrown to the winds: the question ordinary and extraordinary to be first applied in order to obtain revelation of her accomplices.'

She declared in the evening that the part of the sentence which had so startled her at the first reading that she could not hear the rest, was the passage which stated that she was to be put in a cart. Her pride was aroused.

After the sentence had been read, the condemned woman was led into the torture-chamber, and when she saw the apparatus, she said: 'Gentlemen, it is useless, I will tell everything without torture. Not that I think I can escape it—my sentence orders me to be tortured, and I suppose it will not be dispensed with—but I will declare all beforehand. I have denied everything hitherto, because I imagined I was thus defending myself, and that I was not bound to confess anything. I have been convinced of the contrary, and I will behave in accordance with the instructions given me. And I can assure you that if I had seen three weeks ago the person whom I have had given me the last twenty-four hours, you would three weeks ago have known what you are going to learn now.' Then raising her voice, she made a clear and complete avowal of the crimes of her life. As to the composition of the poisons she had employed, she knew only arsenic, vitriol, and the poison of toads. The strongest poison was 'rarefied arsenic.' The only antidote which she had used herself when poisoned by Sainte-Croix was milk. As to her accomplices, apart from Sainte-Croix and her lackeys she declared that she had never had or known any.

The judges were struck by the frankness of her words. And as we know, she spoke at that moment with entire sincerity.

Madame de Brinvilliers underwent the cruelest torture then applied by the Parlement of Paris: the ordeal of water. Enormous quantities of water were introduced into the stomach of the condemned through a funnel placed between the teeth. This water, rapidly accumulating inside the body, produced the most horrible agonies.

Meanwhile the poor abbé Pirot was suffering as much from the torture as the sufferer herself: 'I did not see her from half-past seven until two o'clock in the afternoon. I can say that this was the only bad time I had that day; apart from the time I spent without her, the rest cost me nothing. But while she was under torture I was extraordinarily restless, saying to myself at every moment, "They are now giving her torture."'

He took refuge in a little room where, in spite of the promises of the jailer, he was besieged by importunate visitors. Curious ladies of the court flocked to him. While there some one handed to him a little medal, with a message from the wife of President Lamoignon, saying that she had received it from the pope, with the authority to bestow indulgence on any dying person she chose, and that she gave it to Madame de Brinvilliers.

At last Pirot was told that he would find the marchioness lying on a mattress near the fire. It was a thrilling moment. By his gentle and sympathetic words, and his exhortation to repentance, Pirot had little by little bent this character of iron. He had sent the condemned lady resigned and submissive to the judges. But under the pangs of torture which made strong men yield, under the brutal force she had to suffer, all the pride of her proud nature started up, the worst instincts were awakened. In revenge, she accused Briancourt of false witness; she charged Desgrez, who had arrested her at Liége, with purloining documents. Pirot found her full of hatred and stubbornness, her eyes blazing. 'She was highly excited, her face red as fire, her eyes gleaming, her mouth distorted. She asked for wine, which I had brought to her at once.'

The rest of the story is really touching. The abbé Pirot watched with the care of an anxious mother over the reputation of the lady about to die. 'I expressly notice this circumstance,' he says, 'to undeceive those who believe that she was too fond of wine and was guilty of taking it to excess, and that she could not refrain from drinking it freely on the day of her death. I saw nothing of the kind. It is true that on Thursday, as on Friday, she had a cup from which at times she tasted as much as a fly might swallow; but this was only to keep up her strength and to refresh herself, at a time when the strain of recalling to mind her whole life, in order to assure herself of any criminality there might have been in it, much exhausted and excited her; and if care was taken to have good wine on the day of her death, it was only to cheer her a little in her natural depression of spirits. It has even been cast up against her, unjustly, that a bottle was provided for her on the way to the scaffold: I am responsible for that. I feared that her heart might fail her, and knowing that at one time it was common to offer criminals strong drink of some kind, to give them courage to suffer death, I thought that, as I had seen her necessity that day of refreshing herself now and then, it would be well to have wine ready; and, to tell the truth, I thought a little of myself. The wine was only used by the executioner, who drank a mouthful immediately after the execution.'

Before setting out for her punishment the marchioness was to be allowed to pray for a few moments in the chapel of the Conciergerie, before the Holy Sacrament exposed for the purpose; but she had to appear there surrounded by other prisoners, who were all admitted to the chapel when the Host was placed on the altar. 'When we entered the vestry of the Conciergerie, she asked the jailer for a pin to fasten the kerchief she had on her neck, and as he went in all good faith to look for one, she said to him: "You must not be afraid of anything now: the gentleman will be my surety, and will answer for it that I do not want to do myself harm." "Madam," he replied, giving her a pin, "I beg pardon, I never mistrusted you, and if anybody ever did so, it was certainly not I." He fell on his knees before her, and thus kneeling kissed her hands. She begged him to pray to God for her. "Madam," he replied, his voice choked with sobs, "I will pray for you to-morrow with all my heart."'

'Meanwhile,' says Pirot, 'she had not yet recovered the penitent spirit which I had seen in her that morning and the night before.' She spoke of the sentence. The punishment did not terrify her, but she was bitterly indignant at the degrading circumstances introduced into it—the public penance, the scattering of her ashes to the winds. Pirot replied: 'Madam, it matters nothing to your salvation whether your body be laid in the earth or be cast into the fire. It will rise glorious from the ashes if your soul is in grace.' And further: 'Yes, madam, this flesh which men are soon to burn will rise one day, the same but glorified, provided that your soul rejoices in God; it will be born again, bright as the sun, no more to suffer, subtle and quick as a spirit.'

By degrees Pirot regained his hold upon the fair penitent. 'The cloud of nature was dissolved, her agitation appeared no longer, and, instead of the hard fierce looks, the biting of lips, and the other impetuous manifestations of a shattered pride, there were only tears and sobs, remorse for sin and yearnings for repentance, that would make one's heart bleed. I could not keep back my tears, and for an hour and a half I wept with her, speaking, nevertheless, with more force than I had yet done. She was still more affected by my tears than by my words, and, pondering on the cause of my tears, she said: "Sir, my distress must be great to compel you to weep so much, or you take a great interest in what concerns me."'

Then she confessed the calumnies she had been unable to avoid conceiving under torture against Briancourt and Desgrez. Pirot was alarmed, and when he told her that she ought to repair the fresh sin by a fresh declaration she appeared surprised. However, the opportunity was about to be afforded, for about six o'clock the procurator-general sent for the abbé Pirot.

'Sir,' he said, 'this is a most vexatious woman.'

'How, sir? For my part, I am greatly consoled by the state in which I now see her, and I hope that God will have mercy upon her.'

'Ah, sir! she confesses her crime, but she does not reveal her accomplices.'

Shortly afterwards the procurator-general returned to the chapel along with some commissaries and Drouet the clerk of the court. Pirot repeated to the marchioness what had just been said to him, adding that she could only hope for pardon if she revealed to the judges all she knew. 'Sir,' she said, 'it is true that you told me that at first and at greater length, and I have followed your instructions and know nothing more than I have declared. I have already testified to these gentlemen that you had well instructed me, and it was through that that I told them everything. I have told everything, sir, and have nothing more to say.' Monsieur de Palluau at once said, 'This is more than enough, sir; adieu.' 'He went away at once, and we were given only a short time to spend in that place, the day beginning to decline; it might be about a quarter to seven. I have no doubt she was pretty tired of so much questioning; however, I saw not the shadow of a complaint, so great was her courtesy.' Before the procurator-general and the rest retired, Pirot, with the authority of the prisoner, cleared Briancourt and Desgrez from the accusations brought against them in the torture-chamber.

Madame de Brinvilliers remained a moment longer prostrate before the altar, then went out to meet her doom. At this moment the executioner came up to speak of 'a saddler to whom she owed the balance of the price of a carriage; she told him shortly that she would see to it, and said that very sweetly, but as she would have spoken to a man much inferior to herself.'

As she left the chapel, she stumbled upon some fifty people of rank— the Countess de Soissons, Mademoiselle de Lendovie, Madame de Roquelaure, the Abbé de Chaluset, all jostling one another to see her. Her pride was offended, and after freely staring at them, she said to her confessor: 'Sir, what a strange curiosity!'

She went on, barefooted, clothed in the coarse linen shirt of condemned criminals, holding in one hand the penitent's candle, and in the other a crucifix.

On leaving the Conciergerie she was lifted into the cart. 'It was one of the smaller carts you see in the streets loaded with rubbish; it was very short and narrow, and I feared there was not room enough for her and me. Yet four of us got in, the executioner's assistant sitting on the board which closed it in front, with his feet on the shafts on either side of the horse. She and I sat on the straw put down to cover up the wood, and the executioner stood upright at the back. She got in first, and leant her back against the front-board and against the side, slightly at an angle. I was near her, pressing against her to make room for the executioner's feet, my back against the side of the cart, and my knees doubled up uncomfortably.'

The cart proceeded slowly towards the Place de Grève, which extended from the Hôtel de Ville to the Seine. It was not easy to get through the crowd which pressed around it. The streets were black with people, and the windows crowded with sightseers. At this moment the lady's features underwent a sudden change of expression: 'They were dreadfully convulsed, the keenest agony being expressed in the eyes, and the whole countenance wild.' 'Sir,' she said to her confessor, 'would it be possible, after all that is passing now, for Monsieur de Brinvilliers to have so little feeling as to remain in this world?'

Pirot answered as best he could, endeavouring to ease her mind; but what he said fell on deaf ears, for the marchioness 'then suffered one of the strongest convulsions of her nature in the vivid apprehension of so much shame. Her face contracted, her brows were knitted, her eyes flashed, her mouth was distorted, and her whole aspect was embittered.' 'I do not think,' adds Pirot, 'that there was a moment in all the time that I had been with her when her appearance betokened more indignation, and I am not surprised that Monsieur Le Brun, who is said to have seen her at that spot, where he could look close at her for some minutes, made so fiery and terrible a head as he is said to have done in the portrait he took of her.' Le Brun's sketch is now No. 853 at the exhibition of the Louvre; it is in red and black chalks. It is an admirable drawing, unquestionably the artist's masterpiece. Pirot is sketched in silhouette beside the lady.

As the cart passed slowly through the crowd, voices were raised crying out for blood, and heaping curse on curse; but others spoke pitiful words, and she heard prayers for her salvation. There was a sudden revulsion of opinion in her favour, which grew stronger and stronger till the hour of her death.

The shirt in which she was clothed filled her with amazement. 'Sir,' she said to her confessor, 'look; I am dressed all in white.'

All at once a new contraction marked her features. She had just noticed Desgrez riding near her, the man who had arrested her at Liége, and subjected her to some rough treatment. She asked the executioner to move so as to hide this man from her; then she felt remorse for this 'delicacy,' and asked the executioner to return to his former position. 'It was the last time her countenance showed any grimace,' says Pirot. From that moment she was wholly under the fortifying influence of the priest who assisted her. Hope arose in her soul, more and more clear and radiant, and gave strength to her heart.

She knelt down on the step of the great door of Notre Dame, and there repeated with docility the formula dictated by the executioner, in which she publicly confessed her crimes. 'Some people say that she hesitated in saying her father's name,' observes Pirot; 'but I noticed nothing of the sort.'

Then they remounted the cart to wend towards the Place de Grève. 'Not a word of reproach or complaint against any one escaped her; she showed no sign of vulgar fear. If she dreaded death, it was only in anticipation of the judgment of God, and neither the sight of the Grève, the proximity of the scaffold, nor the appearance of all the terrible apparatus used in this kind of execution gave her the least shadow of fright.'

The cart stopped. The executioner said to her: 'Madam, you must persevere: it is not enough to have come here and to have responded hitherto to what this gentleman has been saying, you must go on to the end as you have begun.' 'This he said in a noticeably humane manner,' observes Pirot, 'and I was edified by it. It is true that she answered never a word, but she courteously bent her head as though to show that she took well what he had said and that she meant to continue in the temper in which he saw her. He confessed to me that he was surprised at her firmness.'

At this moment a clerk of the Parlement appeared. The commissaries were sitting in the Hôtel de Ville ready to receive any declaration Madame de Brinvilliers might still have to make about her accomplices. 'Sir,' she replied, 'I have no more to say; I have told all I know.' She renewed the declaration whereby she freed Briancourt and Desgrez from the accusations fabricated against them at her torture.

The executioner placed the ladder against the scaffold. 'She looked at me,' says Pirot, 'with a gentle countenance and an expression full of gratitude and tenderness, and with tears in her eyes. "Sir," she said to me in a pretty loud tone, which showed how self-possessed she was, but as courteous as it was firm, "we are not yet to separate. You promised not to leave me till my head is off; I hope that you will keep your word." And as I answered nothing, because the tears and sighs which I could only with difficulty restrain robbed me of all power of speech, she added, "I beseech you, sir, to forgive me and not to regret the time you have given to me. I am sorry, for my part, to have given you so little satisfaction, at least at certain moments; I beg your pardon for it. But I cannot die without asking you to say a *De profundis* on the scaffold at the moment of my death, and a mass to-morrow. Remember me, sir, and pray for me."' Pirot remarks, 'If I had not been at that moment more deeply moved than I had ever been in my life, I should have had many things to reply to her courtesies, and I should have promised her more than one mass; but I found it impossible to say anything more than "Yes, madam, I will do all that you bid me."'

Just as she was walking up the steps Madame de Brinvilliers found herself next to Desgrez. She then asked his forgiveness for the trouble she had given him, and begged him to say a few masses and to pray for her. She ended her 'compliment' by saying that 'she was his servant, and so she would die on the scaffold.' Then she added, 'Adieu, sir.'

The throng was immense. Madame de Sévigné, who had come to witness the execution from the window of one of the houses on the bridge Notre Dame, writes: 'Never was such a crowd seen, nor Paris so moved or so eager.'

The marchioness knelt down on the scaffold, her face turned towards the river. 'It was at that moment,' says Pirot, 'that I saw her so intent upon herself, so wholly occupied with what I had said we would do on the scaffold, telling me with such wonderful composure all that was necessary, and making me pass from one thing to another in due order without any prompting from me, wholly absorbed in what I said to her to prepare her for death, without the appearance of any wandering in her thoughts.

'She was absolutely without fear. She was gentle, courteous, steadfast, and self-forgetful. She had very great patience to endure with extraordinary docility all the executioner's preparations. He undid her hair while she was on her knees; he cut it behind and at both sides; to do so he made her turn her head several times in different ways, and he even turned it himself sometimes with no great gentleness: that lasted quite half an hour. She felt keenly the shame of the proceeding in the sight of so great a company; but she overcame her grief and submitted to everything even with joy. I fancy that she had never allowed her hair to be done so quietly as she then let it be cut and shaved; the executioner's hand felt no rougher to her than that of a maid doing her hair; she punctually obeyed his instructions as to turning, lowering, and raising her head when he pleased. He tore off the top of the shirt which he had put over her cloak when she left the Conciergerie, so as to uncover her shoulders. She let him bind her hands as though he were putting on golden bracelets, and knot the rope about her neck as if it had been a necklace of pearls.

MADAME DE BRINVILLIERS
ON THE WAY TO EXECUTION. HER DRESS IS COVERED BY
THE SHIRT WORN BY CONDEMNED CRIMINALS. ON THE
RIGHT IS THE PROFILE OF HER CONFESSOR, THE ABBÉ
PIROT
(From a Sketch by Charles Le Brun, preserved in the Louvre)

"'I should like to be burned alive," she said, "to render my sacrifice more meritorious, if I could have sufficient confidence in my courage to bear that kind of death without falling into despair.'"

The Abbé Pirot chanted the *Salve*, and the people crowding round the scaffold continued the chant that he began. Then he told the lady that he was about to give her absolution. Thereupon she said, her soul at peace, 'Sir, you promised me just now to give me a second penitence on the scaffold, when I pleaded that what you gave me was too easy, and now you say nothing about it.' 'I asked her to say an *Ave* and a *Sancta est Maria mater gratiae*. At the end of which, saying to her, "Madam, renew your contrition," I gave her absolution, saying only the sacramental words because time was pressing.'

The expression of her face was transformed. It was an expression of hope and joy, of serene faith and love, mingled with the exaltation of the penitent. 'Never have I seen anything more touching,' says Pirot, 'than her eyes appeared to me, and if I had to paint a countenance full of contrition and sorrow of heart and hope of pardon, I could wish for no other features than those I remember still, and shall remember all my life long.'

Guillaume the executioner bandaged the eyes of the condemned woman. She repeated the last prayers along with her confessor. Guillaume with the back of his sleeve wiped away the beads of sweat which covered his brow. Suddenly Pirot heard a dull blow, and ceased to speak. 'Madame de Brinvilliers held her head very straight. The executioner severed it at a single stroke, which cut so clean that it remained for a moment on the trunk before falling. I was indeed in agony for an instant, fearing that he had missed his aim and that he would have to strike a second time.'

'Sir,' said the headsman, 'isn't it a fine stroke?'

He added: 'On these occasions I always commend myself to God, and hitherto he has been with me; five or six days ago this lady was troubling me and I couldn't get her out of my head: I will have six masses said.' And, uncorking a bottle, he drank a good draught of wine.

The body was borne to the stake; the flames consumed it, and then the ashes were scattered; but the mob struggled to collect some fragments of the charred bones: all who had been able to get near the scaffold had seen the face of the criminal illumined with a halo, and they departed saying that the dead woman was a saint. Madame de Sévigné writes that Pirot repeated the saying to every one he met.

The children of the Marquis de Brinvilliers took the name of Offémont.

Pennautier was acquitted and left the prison on July 27. He recovered his high position and the repute in which he had been held.

In declaring that she had had no other accomplices than Sainte-Croix and her lackeys Madame de Brinvilliers was speaking the truth. But at that period crimes as great as hers were being committed in Paris, and it was not long before the judges discovered them. There was for instance the celebrated case heard by the 'Chambre Ardente,' to which that of Madame de Brinvilliers serves as introduction.

THE POISON DRAMA AT THE COURT OF LOUIS XIV

I. THE SORCERESSES

The Dinner of La Vigoureux.

THE trial of Madame de Brinvilliers had just caused an immense sensation. The penitentiaries of Notre Dame, without naming any person, declared that 'the majority of those who had confessed to them for some time accused themselves of poisoning somebody.' The court and the city were still disturbed by the catastrophe which had at St. Cloud suddenly carried off the charming Henrietta, Duchess of Orleans, by the sudden death of Hugues de Lionne, the great statesman, and by the startling fate which had just befallen the Duke of Savoy. A note found on September 21, 1677, in the confessional of the Jesuits in Rue Saint-Antoine denounced a plot to poison the king and the dauphin. On December 5 following, La Reynie, lieutenant of police, caused the arrest of Louis de Vanens, who said he had been an officer. The papers seized on him and on Finette, his mistress, brought to light an association of alchemists, coiners, and magicians, in which priests, officers, important bankers like Cadelan were associated with light women, lackeys, and vagabonds. The Parlement was investigating the matter, when La Reynie put his hand on a second association, like the first to all appearance, but soon to reveal itself to the eyes of the magistrates as an affair of much greater importance still.

Towards the end of the year 1678, an advocate in small practice named Maître Perrin was dining in Rue Courtauvilain with a certain Madame Vigoureux, wife of a ladies' tailor—the trade, it will be seen, existed before to-day. The company was merry, and the wine flowed freely. Among the party was a 'big, powerful, large-faced woman,' who choked with laughter as she poured out for herself bumpers of burgundy that would have made a grenadier stagger. Her name was Marie Bosse, and she was the widow of a horse-dealer. She was further a well-known fortune-teller—'devineresse,' as they said in those days. 'A fine trade!' she cried, and spoke of the grand people who frequented her little rookery in the Rue du Grand-Huleu—duchesses and marchionesses and princes and lords. 'Another three poisonings, and she would retire with her fortune made!' At this remark the guests began to laugh still more loudly: this fat woman was irresistibly funny. Maître Perrin alone saw, by a sharp and rapid frown on the face of Madame Vigoureux, that there was something serious in it. He knew Desgrez, the police officer who had arrested Madame de Brinvilliers, and to him he related the incident. Desgrez did not laugh at all, and that very day he sent the wife of one of his archers to the fortune-teller with a complaint against her husband. The fortune-teller, at the first visit, promised her assistance; at the second, she gave her a phial of poison, which the wife at once carried home to her dumfounded husband. La Reynie forthwith ordered the arrest of Madame Vigoureux, of Marie Bosse, with her daughter Manon, and her two sons, one of whom was a soldier in the guards, and the other, a boy of fifteen, was just leaving the workhouse of Bicêtre, where he had been placed to 'improve his morals and give him a taste for work.' Marie Bosse was arrested at her own house on the morning of January 4, 1679, in bed with her two sons. Her daughter had just risen. 'There was only one bed, in which they all slept together.' The preliminary inquiry brought to light a crime, the news of which created a sensation almost as great as that evoked by the poisonings by Madame de Brinvilliers.

An order in council, dated January 10, instructed La Reynie to proceed against the women Bosse, Vigoureux, and their accomplices. On March 12 an officer set about the arrest of Catherine Deshayes, wife of Antoine Monvoisin, a peddling jeweller. This woman, usually known as La Voisin, was the greatest criminal of whom history has any record. She was arrested as she left the church of Notre Dame de Bonne Nouvelle after hearing mass. In her track La Reynie was to penetrate into a region of crime that the imagination can scarcely conceive. 'Human life is publicly trafficked in,' he wrote in utter consternation: 'death is almost the only remedy employed in family embarrassments; impieties, sacrileges, abominations are common practices in Paris, in the country, in the provinces.'

Sorcery in the Seventeenth Century

To understand the facts and the characters of the persons we are going to study, we must dwell briefly upon the beliefs of that time—a time when beliefs were dominant influences in the life of men. We know what power religious sentiments had in the seventeenth century—sentiments of an intensity and a simplicity we know little of to-day, and the corruption of which could not but engender the most absurd superstitions. That was the epoch when the sweet Marguerite Alacoque, in her divine ecstasy, exchanged her heart with that of Christ, and wrote in her own blood, under dictation from on high, the contract which ascribed to God these words: 'I constitute thee heiress of my heart and all its treasures for time and eternity; I promise thee that thou shalt only lack succour when I lack power; thou shalt be for ever the well-beloved disciple, the plaything of my good pleasure and the burnt-offering of my love.' And that, too, was the period when Catherine Monvoisin, the terrible sorceress of Villeneuve-sur-Gravois, found numerous and ardent followers.

The beliefs in the action of the devil, and in the power of the sorcerers, so deeply rooted in the imagination of the seventeenth century, were summed up in 1588 in the *Démonomanie des Sorciers* of the famous Jean Bodin. He defined the sorcerer as one who 'by devilish and unlawful means endeavours to attain some end'; but in his book he speaks for the most part of witches. As Sprenger, the German inquisitor, remarked, 'We should talk of the heresy of the witches, and not of sorcerers, for these are of little account.' In Bodin are to be found most of the practices in black magic still flourishing at the end of the seventeenth century. Sorcerers and witches formed a sort of vast fraternity. There were entire families whose formulae and whose customers were handed down as heritable property. Jeanne Harvillier, burnt to death on April 30, 1579, may serve as type. Her mother, a witch like herself, had been burnt to death thirty years before. Such a death was the natural end to her career, an end foreseen, and one that terrified those fascinated by the strange vocation much less than one would imagine. Jeanne was born about 1528, at Verberie near Compiègne. At the age of twelve she was presented by her mother to the devil, who appeared to her in the shape of a very tall dark man. Jeanne renounced God, and consecrated herself to the 'Spirit.' 'At the same time she had carnal intercourse with him, which continued from the age of twelve to the age of fifty, when she was arrested. It sometimes happened that her husband, lying by her side, failed to perceive what was going on.' This was the *incubat*. Jeanne Harvillier was brought to justice on the charge of causing the death of men and beasts by witchcraft. She confessed to it with the greatest frankness, and told the story of her last homicide: 'She laid some powders, prepared for her by the devil, in the place where the man who had beaten his daughter was to pass.' Another man came by to whom she wished no harm, and immediately he felt a sharp pain all over his body. She promised to cure him, and in fact took her place at the bedside of the sick man and tended him with the gentleness of a sister of mercy. She fervently besought the devil to restore life to the dying man, but the devil replied that it was impossible.

Bodin gravely recounts how witches on the Sabbath flew through the air on broomsticks. He adds: 'What we have said of the travels of the witches, both in body and in spirit, and the frequent and memorable experiences of the same, show as in broad daylight, and bring to the test of touch and sight, the error of those who have written that the flights of witches are imaginary, and nothing but a trance.' This last opinion had been maintained by John Wier, physician to the Duke of Cleves, in a book which is almost a work of genius for that period. Bodin devoted all his energy to its refutation, for to throw any doubt upon the fact that the devil transports witches from one place to another would be, he said, to bring gospel history into ridicule.

Coming to study the maladies attributed to the incantations of sorcerers—consumption, hysteria, melancholy, delusions, debility—John Wier found the remedies to consist in a regular life, in conformity with the laws of God, and in the skill of physicians. What an abominable doctrine! says Bodin. He had lost all respect, then, for anything. Bodin was beside himself. John Wier, he says, wrote under the dictation of Satan. Moreover, had he not himself confessed that he was a disciple of Agrippa, 'the greatest sorcerer that ever was'? When Agrippa died in the hospital of Grenoble, a black dog which he called 'Monsieur' instantly went and sprang into the river. Wier declared, it is true, that this dog was not the devil, but there was not a single sensible person who believed him.

Without taking a side in this famous dispute between Bodin and John Wier, we are bound to state that the writings of the latter had no success, at any rate in France, while Bodin's book became a classic. Bossuet, for all his powerful intellect, firmly believed in sorcery. At the close of the seventeenth century, Bonet was obliged to go to a Protestant republic to get his treatise on medicine printed, in which he spoke lightly of magic and demoniacal possession. We have to come far into the eighteenth century to find one Abraham de Saint-André—and he was physician to Louis XV— daring, in his famous *Letters*, to cast doubt on the magic and witchcraft of sorcerers.

The following case, tried at the period in which the events of our story occurred, and reproduced here after the archives of the Bastille, will enable us to understand the ardour of belief with which the sorcerers themselves were animated.

By sentence of the Tournelle on September 2, 1687, a certain Pierre Hocque was condemned to the galleys. He was a shepherd, skilled in magic, who had, as the judgment declared, caused the death, by a spell he cast over them, of 395 sheep, 7 horses, and 11 cows belonging to Eustache Visié, receiver of taxes at Pacy-en-Brie. Hocque was chained up with the other galley prisoners. Nevertheless, the cattle of Eustache Visié continued to die. He had no sooner bought a cow or a sheep and placed it in his farm than it perished. Clearly the only remedy was to get Pierre Hocque to remove the direful spell he had imposed. Visié won over, by a promise of money, the galley prisoner who was fastened to the chain next to Hocque—a man named Béatrix. He spoke to the shepherd, who replied that he had in fact cast a poison-spell over the cattle of Visié, and that, failing himself, only two shepherds named Bras-de-Fer and Courte Epée had the power to remove the fatal charm. At the urgent request of Béatrix, Hocque dictated a letter to be sent to Bras-de-Fer, but the letter was no sooner despatched than he fell into a horrible despair. He cried hoarsely that Béatrix had made him do something that would cause his death, which he would be unable to escape from the moment Bras-de-Fer began to raise the spell he had cast on the cattle. And the unhappy wretch writhed about in such dreadful contortions that the other prisoners would have murdered Béatrix but for the intervention of the guards. The despair and the convulsions lasted for several days, and then Hocque died. 'And it was the exact time,' says the official document, 'when Bras-de-Fer began to exorcise the cattle.' The judges add: 'It is established that Pierre Hocque died because Bras-de-Fer removed the poison-spell from the horses and cows, and it is true that since that time no more of Eustache Visié's horses and cows have died.'

The conviction of the unhappy sorcerer that he was bound to die as soon as his mate undid his work was so strong that he did die. Is it possible to imagine a more striking proof of the robust faith people then had in all these devilries?

The practices of the Witches

To magic, black or white, the witches added medicine and pharmacy. They kept drugstores with phials innumerable: syrups, juleps, ointments, balms, emollients in infinite variety. They were old wives' remedies, but their efficacy had been proved by experience, and their preparation was perfected from age to age. Paracelsus, the great Renaissance physician, burnt in 1527 the medical books of his time, declaring that nothing but the formulae of the witches was of any use. The old hags had soothing draughts for pain, healing ointments for wounds, and they acted on nervous maladies by suggestion. That was the serious side of their art. Most often the witch was a midwife too; but just as in that strange world the poisoner lurked behind the druggist, and the alchemist and the coiner were one, so the midwife played the part of baby-farmer. Finally, the witches were fortune-tellers, who cast one's horoscope according to the drawing of cards or the lines of the hand.

What were the declarations of the witches arrested by La Reynie? Marie Bosse said that 'nothing better could be done than to exterminate all that sort of people who examine the hand, because they are the ruin of many a woman, women of quality as well as others; the fortune-teller soon finds out their weak spot, and thereby knows how to take them and lead them wherever she will.' She added that in Paris there were more than 400 fortune-tellers and magicians 'who ruined a great many people, especially women, and of all conditions.' She went on to speak of the money her cronies earned, telling how they bought places for their husbands and built houses, and that they did not realise such fortunes merely by looking at people's hands. La Voisin said that nothing could be better than to hunt up all the people who looked at hands, that those engaged in the business 'heard strange things when love intrigues were not prospering, that poisonings were an everyday occurrence, that many of them were paid as much as 10,000 livres' (£2000 of our money). Similar declarations were made by Leroux, another witch, and by the magician Lesage. 'It is extremely important,' said the latter, 'to get to the bottom of these wretched practices, and to fathom this mystery of iniquity which exists among all those who ostensibly are seekers after treasure, after the philosopher's stone, and other like things, but who keep up their trade by very different means: abortions and other crimes are greater treasures than the philosopher's stone and fortune-telling; the people who apply to the workers in mystery discuss usually the poisoning of a husband, or a wife, or a father, and even sometimes of babies at the breast.' He went on to say that 'these wretched people had obtained the protection of very powerful friends, so that they acted with perfect assurance and in almost perfect freedom.' These statements are confirmed by the documents La Reynie was able to get together.

What the public asked of the witches was, first of all, to withdraw the veil from the future, and then to enable them to discover treasures. For this purpose various means were employed, all tending to the same end—to compel the 'Spirit,' that is the devil, by charms and incantations to present himself and reveal the mysterious spot where treasures lay hid. 'A woman,' writes Ravaisson, 'usually a prostitute on the eve of accouchement, was placed at the centre of a circle drawn on the floor, and surrounded with dark candles; when the child was born, the mother gave up her son to be consecrated to the devil. After pronouncing filthy incantations, the priest cut the victim's throat, sometimes under the very eyes of its mother; but more often he carried it away to sacrifice it elsewhere, because at the last moment outraged nature asserted her rights, and these unhappy creatures snatched their babes from death. At other times, they were content to cut the throat of a deserted child; of such there was no lack; imprudent girls, light women, gave the witches authority to dispose of the fruits of an unlawful love. There were even licensed midwives who did a large business in procuring abortion; the children after being baptized were put to death and carried at once to the cemetery; most often they were buried in the corner of a wood or consumed in an oven.' And the witch Marie Bosse added: 'There are so many of this sort of people in Paris that the city is choke-full of them.'

These were the practices, with others more abominable still, which caused La Reynie to write: 'It is difficult to think merely that these crimes are possible; one can hardly bring oneself to consider them. Yet it is those who have committed them that themselves declare them, and these villains give so many particulars that it is difficult to harbour any doubt.'

The Alchemists

Alongside of the group of witches and magicians appears another group, that of the alchemists and 'philosophers,' represented by such people as Vanens, Chasteuil, Cadelan, Rabel, and Bachimont. We have mentioned the arrest of Louis de Vanens on December 5, 1677.

The origins of this association of alchemists and seekers after the philosopher's stone were highly dramatic. François Galaup de Chasteuil, second of the name—he belonged to an illustrious family of Languedoc, which had produced men of the highest distinction in arms, religion, and literature—was its chief, or to use the cant expression of the cabala, its 'author.' His life had been more than ordinarily romantic. Born at Aix, on November 15, 1625, he was the second son of Jean Galaup de Chasteuil, attorney-general of the Exchequer Court of Aix. His elder brother Hubert, solicitor-general to the Parlement of the same town, was 'renowned for the nobility of his mind and the profundity of his knowledge'; his younger brother Pierre was a poet, the friend of Boileau, La Fontaine, and Mademoiselle de Scudéry. After a successful student career, François was admitted doctor of law. In 1644 he became a knight of Malta. He did signal service to the Order, and Lascaris, the grand master, placed on his breast the cross of honour. He then became captain of the guards of the great Condé. In 1652 he retired to Toulon, fitted out a ship, and under the Maltese flag went privateering against the Mussulmans. Algerian corsairs captured him and led him into captivity. After two years of slavery he came to Marseilles, where he turned monk and became prior of the Carmelites. He smuggled into the convent a young girl—a slender, fair-haired child, with large, bright blue eyes; and there he kept her locked up in his cell. When she was on the point of giving birth to her child, Chasteuil, assisted by a lay brother, strangled her in her bed, and on a pitch-dark night carried her into the chapel of the convent, where he lifted several slabs of the floor and dug out a grave in which to bury her. The silence of the arches was disturbed by a dull sound. A pilgrim, lying asleep against a pillar, woke up, and saw the sinister toilers by the light of the moon which shone through the stained windows. Transfixed with fright, he remained hidden out of sight in a dark corner until dawn, when the chapel was opened, and he ran to inform the magistrates. Chasteuil was arrested, tried, and condemned. He was on the way to execution when, at the foot of the gibbet, up came Louis de Vanens, captain of the galleys, along with several soldiers. Chasteuil and Vanens were old friends. Chasteuil was rescued, and, taking his rescuer with him, he fled to Nice.

Hiding in a quiet spot, the two friends began working at the philosopher's stone, that is, at converting copper into silver and gold. Chasteuil had some experience of alchemy, and fancied he was master of the famous secret. Full of gratitude for the service done him, he gave

Vanens the secret so far as silver was concerned, but would tell him nothing about the gold, 'not thinking Vanens prudent enough for that.' Shortly afterwards we find Chasteuil in the service of the Duke of Savoy, captain of the guards of the White Cross, and—extraordinary fact—tutor to his son! While occupied with the education of the young Prince of Piedmont, Chasteuil continued his 'philosophy,' and discovered an oil, which, as he appeared convinced himself, would turn metals into gold. He also wrote translations of authors sacred and profane—the minor prophets, Petronius, the Thebaïd of Statius; and he dabbled in poetry. He had just passed his fortieth year. A contemporary gives us his portrait: 'Middle height, very thin, always troubled with a nasty cough caused by a wound he received in the body, round-shouldered, slightly crooked, with a wry mouth, scanty beard, hair black and flat, complexion swarthy and sallow.' Moréri adds: 'Monsieur de Chasteuil was one of the most accomplished of gentlemen, and a perfect master of the platonic philosophy.'

Vanens and Chasteuil struck up an alliance with Robert de Bachimont, lord of La Miré, who had married a cousin of Superintendent Fouquet. Bachimont had at Paris a house near the Temple, with four smelting furnaces: a large one on the third floor, two smaller ones in an ante-room, and a large one in the cellar. He also had apartments at Compiègne in the *Ecu de France*, where there was nothing but crucibles, alembics, vessels of glass and of earthenware, cucurbits, philosophical stoves open and closed, grates and mortars, retorts and matrasses, sal-ammoniac and iron filings, and a thousand varieties of powders, pastes, and liquids. Finally, he had another establishment at the abbey of Ainay, near Lyons, completely fitted up for the fusion of metals, the distillation of herbs, and other practices of alchemy. Before long the association was enlarged by the addition of a person of some importance, Louis de Vasconcelos y Souza, Count of Castelmelhor, who had been practically the governor of Portugal for five or six years as the favourite of King Alfonso VI. Bachimont says that Castelmelhor taught him the secret of colouring glass red. After the death of the Duke of Savoy on June 12, 1675, Castelmelhor withdrew to England, where he gained the favour of Charles II., an ardent alchemist and astrologer. He was present at the death of the English king, and it was he that brought in the Catholic priest who gave him extreme unction.

Chasteuil and his partners spent their time in the quest for the philosopher's stone, contact with which was to convert metals into gold; and, like the majority of alchemists, they believed that it was to be found in the solidification of mercury. 'The hermetic philosophers,' writes M. Huysmans, 'discovered—and modern science to-day does not deny that they were right—that the metals are compound bodies of identical composition. Their varieties are due simply to the different proportions of the elements in combination; it is possible then, by the aid of an agent that would alter these proportions, to change these bodies one into another—to transmute mercury, for instance, into silver, and lead into gold. And this agent is the philosopher's stone, mercury: not ordinary mercury, which, to alchemists, is only a bastard metal' (M. Huysmans uses another expression), 'but the mercury of the philosophers, called also *lion vert*.'

Among the papers of La Voisin was found an MS. poem in honour of the philosopher's stone:

'De l'or glorifié qui change en or ses frères.'

The secret consisted in an elixir, of which a single drop, cast

'dans une mer profonde
Où couleraient fondus tous les métaux du monde,
Suffirait pour la teindre et fixer en soleil.'[7]

Chasteuil and his fellows did not merely seek the solidification of mercury, which was to produce the philosopher's stone, but the liquefaction of gold by cold: this was to furnish a universal panacea. 'Liquid gold restores health and strength, gives flesh to greybeards and colour to the cheeks of girls, cures the plague,' and so on.

Solid mercury being unobtainable, they sought, for the transmutation of metals, those powders or oils about which we hear so frequently at that period; and, as we shall see, they had the best reasons in the world for believing that they had put their finger on the secret, at least as far as silver[8] was concerned.

In 1676 our partners all established themselves at Paris, where they added to their company three collaborators, all important in different ways: the quack Rabel, a physician celebrated in his day; a rich banker of Paris named Pierre Cadelan, secretary to the king; and a young Parlement advocate named Jean Terron du Clausel. Du Clausel lodged with Vanens in the Rue d'Anjou, in a house which had for sign *Le Petit Hôtel d'Angleterre*. He was a valuable addition to the band, because he could distil at pleasure, being 'licensed.' Rabel seems to have been possessed of considerable real science. Rabel water, which he invented, is still used in our own day—a mixture of alcohol and sulphuric acid, which acts as an astringent in cases of hæmorrhage. Rabel had compounded another elixir, whose innumerable merits were celebrated in notices in prose and verse which the most glowing of modern advertisements have not surpassed. Cadelan supplied funds. Bodin speaks in very precise terms about the alchemists: 'They extract the quintessence of plants, and make admirable and salutary oils and waters, and discourse subtly on the virtues and the transmutation of metals; but they also make false money.' At the moment when Cadelan and his associates were arrested, he was on the point of farming the Paris mint. Was this in order to make false *louis d'or*, as historians have supposed? We believe rather that it was to find means of circulating the products of the alchemical experiments of his associates, for by that time they had no manner of doubt about the efficacy of Chasteuil's formulae. A bar of silver cast by Vanens, and taken by Bachimont to the mint, had just been accepted there at a good price as pure metal. It is scarcely necessary to add that this could only have been due to an error of the mint official; this famous silver made out of copper by Vanens and Chasteuil was nothing but 'white metal.' Nevertheless, it was a success which opened before the eyes of our partners splendid vistas of future wealth.

When Louis de Vanens was arrested on December 5, 1677, Louvois believed that he had seized a spy. But he had put his hand on an alchemist, and soon the whole band—Terron, Cadelan, Monsieur and Madame Bachimont, Barthomynat (known as La Chaboissière), de Vanens' valet— were laid by the heels, some in the Bastille, the others at Pierre-en-Cize. Chasteuil had just died quietly at Verceil. Rabel had escaped into England, where Charles II lodged and fed him, gave him a pension, and loaded him with presents. Later he returned to France, and was incarcerated in his turn.

We regarded it as essential to say something of this band of alchemists and 'philosophers' by way of introduction to Louis de Vanens. This young noble of Provence, 'a man of well-knit and graceful figure,' had brilliant connections at court, where he was on a footing of intimacy with the king's dazzling mistress, Madame de Montespan. On the other hand, he was an assiduous visitor to La Voisin, and was even for some time her 'author.' Vanens was the link between the alchemists and the witches. He was devoted to demoniacal practices. His valet, La Chaboissière, declared that one night he had to accompany his master and a cleric into the woods on the outskirts of Poissy, where they searched for treasures with incantations and invocations to the 'spirit.' Vanens was a diabolical character. He was confined at the Bastille in the same room with other prisoners, as the custom was. He had with him a sort of white and tan spaniel. As midnight approached, he recited some prayer over the body of the dog, and went through the ceremony of consecration. Then he took a prayer-book containing a picture of the Virgin, and laid the picture on the back of the dog, saying, 'Avaunt, devil! Behold thy good mistress!' To the remarks of his companions in captivity, he replied: 'Neither God nor the king shall prevent me from doing what I have done.' To gauge the strange and passionate vigour of these superstitions, we must remember that Vanens was in the Bastille, quite aware that these practices might bring him to the stake.

We shall see in the sequel the importance of Vanens when we recall the following lines found in the notes of Nicolas de la Reynie: 'To see La Chaboissière again about his reluctance to have written down in his statement, after hearing it read, that Vanens had been concerned in giving Madame de Montespan counsel which deserves that he should be drawn and quartered.'

La Voisin

To the portraits of Chasteuil the alchemist and of Vanens, we must add that of the most famous of the witches, Catherine Deshayes, known as La Voisin. It was of her that La Fontaine wrote:

'Une femme à Paris faisait la pythonisse.'

La Voisin stated to La Reynie: 'Some women asked if they would not soon become widows, because they wished to marry some one else; almost all asked this and came for no other reason. When those who come to have their hands read ask for anything else, they nevertheless always come to the point in time, and ask to be ridded of some one; and when I gave those who came to me for that purpose my usual answer, that those they wished to be rid of would die when it pleased God, they told me that I was not very clever.' Margot, La Voisin's servant, said that the whole world came there, adding: 'La Voisin is to-day dragging a great ruck down with her—a long chain of persons of all sorts and conditions.' The Parisians used to go in companies to the house of the fortune-teller: they were quite pleasure parties. The merry crew would overflow into the garden lawns surrounding the cottage at Villeneuve-sur-Gravois. This was the district, but sparsely inhabited, between the ramparts and the St. Denis quarter.

The sorceress was brought into the city drawing-rooms as nowadays fashionable singers are brought. 'At that time, La Voisin had as much money as she wanted. Every morning, before she rose, people were waiting for her, and she had visitors all the rest of the day: after that, in the evening, she kept open house, engaged fiddlers, and enjoyed herself thoroughly; this went on for several years.' This life had little resemblance, it will be seen, to that of her ancestress, the witch described by Michelet: 'You will find her in the most dismal places, isolated,—in houses of ill-fame and ruined huts and hovels. Where could she have lived except on wild heaths—the hapless wretch who was so hunted down, the accursed, proscribed, hated poisoner?'

La Voisin earned in a year as much as £2000 or even £4000 in English money; but her gains were spent in revelry. She entertained her lovers in princely style, for she would have thought it unworthy of her if they were not comfortable; and her lovers were many. We find in the first rank of them André Guillaume, the executioner of Paris, who beheaded Madame de Brinvilliers, and who, by a horrible coincidence, only just escaped executing La Voisin herself: among them also the Viscount de Cousserans, the Count de Labatie, Fauchet the architect, a wine merchant of the neighbourhood, Lesage the magician, the alchemist Blessis, and others.

We must add that Blessis and Lesage spent much money on her, ostensibly in connection with the philosopher's stone, for La Voisin had a sincere faith in alchemy. She subsidised great enterprises, and helped to establish manufactures, being much interested in scientific and industrial progress; but in regard to industrial undertakings she fell mainly into the hands of sharpers who swindled her out of her money.

However, La Voisin, proud of her trade as sorceress, which brought persons of the highest rank to bend before her in obsequious and suppliant attitudes, did not stick at any expense that seemed likely to augment her glory. She delivered her oracular sayings clothed in a robe and a cloak specially woven for her, for which she paid 15,000 livres (£3000 of English money). The queen herself had no finery more beautiful than this 'imperial robe,' which 'was the talk of all Paris.' The cloak was of crimson velvet studded with 205 two-headed eagles of fine gold, lined with costly fur; the skirt was of bottle-green velvet, edged with French point. Even her shoes were embroidered with golden two-headed eagles. The mere weaving of the eagles on the cloak cost 400 livres (£80 to-day). We possess the bills of the maker.

But under the glittering shows of wealth La Voisin had preserved most dissolute manners. She was constantly drunk. She indulged in fishwife's brawls with Lesage. Latour, who was her 'great author,' used to thrash her. She fought with Marie Bosse and tore her hair out. 'One day, Latour being with her on the ramparts, she got him to give her husband fifty blows with a stick, while she held Latour's hat.' On that occasion, Latour bit poor Monvoisin's nose. But on the other hand, the sorceress regularly attended the church of the Abbé de Saint-Amour, rector of the University of Paris, an austere Jansenist; and Madame de la Roche-Guyon stood god-mother to her daughter.

The husband whom La Voisin so brutally got beaten, appears to have been a decent man. In those days there was at Montmartre a chapel dedicated to St. Ursula, who enjoyed the power to 'improve' husbands. The procedure was to carry there, some Friday morning, a shirt of the wicked spouse. Our sorceress had the most implicit faith in the efficacy of this practice, and we must do her the justice to state that she always began by sending to Montmartre women who came to her with tales of their troubles. She availed herself of the remedy on her own account, and poor Monvoisin had to march to the place carrying his shirt under his arm. He was a husband for whose improvement St. Ursula does not appear to have been required to spend much effort.

Lesage, the witch's lover, advised her to get rid of Monvoisin. A sheep's heart was bought, 'to which Lesage did something,' and then it was buried in the garden behind the gate. Lo and behold, Monvoisin was seized with severe pain in the stomach. He cried out that if there was anybody who wished to do for him, he had better shoot him at once instead of letting him linger. La Voisin, struck with remorse, hastened to the Augustines to confess and obtain a general absolution; she took the sacrament, and on her return compelled Lesage to undo his wicked charms.

She related very simply and frankly to La Reynie the first steps of her career. Her husband, at that time, was doing nothing, but he had been a hawking jeweller, and then a shopkeeper on the Pont-Marie. He had lost his shop, and then, seeing her husband ruined, 'she had devoted herself to cultivating the powers that God had given her.' 'It was chiromancy and face-reading that I learnt at the age of nine. I have been persecuted for fourteen years: that is the work of the missionaries' (these were the members of a community established by St. Vincent de Paul, then very popular, who were actively occupied in converting sinners and removing scandals of all kinds). 'However,' she continued, 'I gave an account of my art to the vicars-general, the Holy See being vacant, and to several doctors of the Sorbonne to whom I had been sent, and they found nothing to object to.' Marie Bosse also spoke of the time when her friend went to the Sorbonne to argue on astrology with the professors.

Thus La Voisin set up as fortune-teller in order to restore order and comfort to her household. One of her friends, La Lepère, told her sometimes that she ought not to engage in such great crimes. 'You are mad!' cried the witch, 'the times are too bad. How am I to feed my family? I have six persons on my hands!' And in fact, until her arrest, La Voisin had been the constant support of her old mother, to whom she gave money every week.

La Voisin's claim that her art was founded on face-reading was quite genuine. She had made a profound study of physiognomy. We find innumerable references to this subject in the documents of her case, and also a 'Treatise on physiognomy, supported on six immovable columns: (1)

sympathy between body and mind; (2) relations between rational and irrational animals; (3) the differences between the sexes; (4) national diversities; (5) physical temperaments; (6) diversities of age; not depending on a single sign, for men are often attacked by some defect which force of mind, aided by grace, can assuredly overcome.' When the Countess de Beaufort de Canillac came to consult the fortune-teller, 'the lady wishing to give me her hand without unmasking, I told her that I did not know physiognomies of velvet, whereupon the lady removed her mask.' La Voisin confessed that she read much more in the features than in the lines of the hand, 'it being no easy thing to conceal a passion or any considerable disturbing emotion.' She was not merely a physiognomist, but an expert psychologist, and that was how she gave a real foundation to her sorcery. We may cite the following incident among many others.

Marie Brissart, widow of a Parlement counsellor, tenderly loved and handsomely supported a captain of guards named Louis Denis de Rubentel, Marquis de Mondétour, who became lieutenant-general in 1688. He was a personage of whom Saint-Simon, a severe censor, speaks thus: 'He had been able to contemn basenesses, and to withdraw into his virtue, which was beyond his wealth.' Madame Brissart used to send him money when he was on service, after having equipped him from top to toe on his departure. It happened that the cavalier displayed some coldness towards his mistress, with the idea of getting her purse to open still more generously. The widow, seeing nothing of her captain, became alarmed, and hastened to La Voisin. She began her incantations, with the assistance of Lesage. The magician walked up and down the garden with a wand, with which he struck the earth, repeating the words, *Per Deum sanctum, per Deum vivum!* Then he said: 'Louis Denis de Rubentel, I conjure thee in the name of the Almighty to go find Marie Miron (Madame Brissart's maiden name): she to possess thee wholly, body, soul, and spirit, and thou to love none but her!' On another occasion, he put into a little ball of wax a paper on which the names of Rubentel and Madame Brissart were written, and in the presence of the latter threw the ball into the fire, where it burst with a loud noise. These fine charms were still without result, when one morning La Voisin, with the intuition of a clairvoyant, said to her weeping client: 'You write every day and send your maid to Rubentel, but he pays no attention to you; it is mad conduct to write and send every day'; and the lady having ceased to write and send, Monsieur de Rubentel, who in turn began to be afraid lest so precious a fount should dry up, returned to her 'without anything else having been done; yet the lady, believing that La Voisin had done some extraordinary thing, gave her twelve pistoles.'

The witch heard all sorts of confessions. There were wonderful dreams of adoring affection told her by lovers of twenty years, who came to her red with emotion, or wrote thrilling letters in order to bring their torment to an end, begging her to soften the hard hearts of their mistresses, or to bend the opposition of a cruel father. Or it was the fierce carnal love of mature women obstinately clinging to the lovers who were neglecting them for fresher girls. There were also the passions of ambitious women, greedy for money and honours, which bring us to the horrors of the 'black mass.'

La Voisin was assisted in these monstrous rites by a priest 'squint-eyed and old,' with bloated face, and prominent blue veins forming a network on his cheeks—the terrible Abbé Guibourg. Formerly chaplain to the Count de Montgommery, he was at this time sacristan of St. Marcel, at St. Denis. He used to say mass, according to the proper rites, wearing the alb, stole, and maniple. 'The women on whose bodies mass was said were laid stark naked, without even their chemise, upon a table which served as altar; their arms were stretched out, and they held a taper in each hand.' Sometimes they did not actually undress themselves, 'but only tucked up their garments as high as the throat.' The chalice was placed on the bare belly. At the moment of the *offertoire*, a child had its throat cut. Guibourg usually stuck a long needle into its neck. The blood of the expiring victim was poured into the chalice, and mixed with the blood of bats and other materials obtained by filthy means. Flour was added to solidify the mess, which was thus made to resemble the Host, to be consecrated at the moment when, in the sacrifice of the mass, transubstantiation takes place. The scene is reconstructed by La Reynie according to the testimony of the accused.

Black masses were not the only sorceries whose rites required the sacrifice of children. La Voisin and her fellow-witches perpetrated a terrible slaughter of them. Children deserted by their unmarried mothers, others bought from poor women, did not suffice: several sorceresses were convicted of having killed their own children for these atrocious proceedings. Here, for instance, is a horrible detail: the daughter of La Voisin, on the very eve of her trouble, not trusting her mother, fled the house, and only returned after placing her infant in safety. The witches ran off with children in the streets. La Reynie wrote to Louvois: 'Remember the great disturbance in Paris in 1676, when there were seditious gatherings and mobs and runnings to and fro in several parts of the city, through the rumour that people carried off children to cut their throats, though no one then understood what the cause of the rumour could be. The mob, however, proceeded to various excesses against the women suspected of being child-stealers. The king ordered an inquiry. Proceedings were taken (against those who rose against the witches), and a woman who was guilty of violence was condemned to death, but obtained a special pardon.'

La Voisin, like all the sorceresses, practised medicine. Among her papers were found recipes for the cure of pimples, a remedy for headache, the prescription for 'a quintessence of hellebore which kept the Dean of Westminster alive for 166 years.' She was a midwife, and especially a procurer of abortion. 'Above the room (where she gave consultations) there was a sort of loft in which she procured abortions, and behind the room there was a recess with a stove, in which were found the charred remains of small human bones.' Little children were burned in this stove. One day, in an effusive moment, La Voisin confessed that 'she had burnt in the stove, or buried in the garden, the bodies of more than 2500 children prematurely born.' Here again we come upon surprising particulars. The witch was very insistent that children thus brought into the world should be baptized before death. One evening La Lepère, a midwife friend of La Voisin, happened to be in the famous room with the witch's husband. La Voisin, who was in the loft, came down suddenly in joyous haste and with radiant countenance, crying: 'What luck! the child has been dipped!'

Such was the strange and horrible creature—the last of the great sorceresses who haunted the imagination of Michelet—the extraordinary woman whose crimes sent a shudder through the man who had heard the confessions of the most redoubtable criminals of his time—Nicolas de la Reynie.

We have a portrait of La Voisin by Antoine Coypel. She is represented on the way to execution in the linen shift of condemned criminals. Contemporaries depict her as a small stoutish woman, rather pretty, owing to her eyes, which were extraordinarily bright and piercing. The artist has given her a froglike expression, but no doubt he sketched her under the influence of a preconceived idea. Madame de Sévigné, who had a singular taste for this sort of spectacle, saw her mount to the stake: 'La Voisin,' she wrote, 'very prettily surrendered her soul to the devil.' The confessor of the sorceress has given his testimony to her edifying end: 'I am loaded with so many crimes,' she said with simple and profound emotion, 'that I could not wish God to work a miracle to snatch me from the flames, because I cannot suffer too much for the sins I have committed.'

The Magician Lesage

La Voisin's principal coadjutor was the magician Lesage. He was one by himself in this world of sorceresses, alchemists, and magicians. A sceptic among believers, he duped the women with whom he worked as well as the fashionable ladies who came to avail themselves of his art.

Originally from Venoix near Caen, his real name was Adam Cœuret. His portrait is sketched by La Vigoureux: 'he wore a ruddy wig, was ill formed, clothed as a rule in grey, with a cloak of homespun.' He was a wool merchant. Though he had a wife in Lower Normandy, he promised La Voisin that he would marry her if she became a widow. The first alias he chose was Duboisson. In 1667 he was arrested, condemned to the galleys for dealings with the devil, and liberated in 1672 through the kind offices of La Voisin. The galley in which he rowed was lying in sight of the port of Genoa when the pardon reached him.

Set at liberty, Cœuret returned to Paris, where he renewed his relations with the witches.

His whole art consisted in a remarkable talent for jugglery, by which he deceived the witches themselves, persuading them that he possessed 'all the science of the cabala.' They adopted him as partner in their lucrative operations. The reports of the examination of La Voisin give curious information on this head. 'Lesage took a live pigeon in the Vale of Misery (on the quay of La Mégisserie, where poultry was sold) and burnt it in a warming-pan. Having then sifted its ashes, he put them in his room. It was the beginning of Lent, during which he used to recite the Passion of our Lord daily, with his feet in water, though it was freezing hard. Then he put a white cloth on the table, lit two tapers, and sent for three crystal glasses, with which having performed his "mystery," which was Greek to La Voisin, he shut them up in a cupboard with a twig of laurel, and then, though he retained the key, he asked her for the three glasses and the laurel twig which he had locked in the cupboard. They were not found there; and then he said that he would give her nothing else to keep, and having sent her into the garden, she found them all three in a row in the summer-house. And when she asked him how he did that, Lesage said that he was one of the apostles and of the company of the Sibyls.'

At other times Lesage celebrated a sort of mass, got up as a priest. At the moment of the offertory he would break two pieces of ordinary bread, and after having made La Voisin and her husband kneel down, he gave them each a piece of bread 'just as if they were at communion, and then made them drink some holy water which, as he said, he had turned into wine, and it was a liquid of an extremely pleasant taste.' 'A sergeant having come to La Voisin's house to distrain on her at the instance of an upholsterer named Lenoir, La Voisin sent for Lesage, told him that she was ruined, and that there was something in the cupboard which must be taken away, namely, a consecrated wafer; and at the same time Lesage sent away the Marquise de Lusignan, who happened to be in the house, and told her to go home, and when she got there to put a white napkin on her bed, for something he was going to send her. And in fact the wafer was found by the marquise at her own house, without any one seeing who had taken it there.'

The pretended sorceries of Lesage thus consisted simply of clever conjuring tricks. They sufficed to amaze his clients. He made them write, for instance, requests to the devil in notes which he then pretended to throw in the fire, enclosed in balls of wax; and some days after he gave them back to them, saying that the devil, who had received them through the flames, had returned them.

Lesage was arrested for the second time on March 17, 1679, and we shall see the importance of the statements he made to the magistrates.

The 'Chambre Ardente'

The consternation of Louis XIV, his ministers, and the lieutenant of police at the discovery of such crimes may be imagined. The terror was all the intenser because chemists and able physicians were then powerless to discover traces of poison in a corpse. The matter was intrusted to a special commission, in the hope that by a more expeditious and energetic procedure than that of the ordinary courts, it would succeed in cutting the evil at the root. This was the famous Chambre Ardente.

The president was Louis Boucherat, Count de Compans—an amiable man, says Madame de Sévigné, and of much good sense. Later, he became Chancellor of France. Louis Bazin, Lord of Bezons, nominated to act as judge-advocate along with La Reynie, was a member of the Academy. The office of clerk was filled by Sagot, La Reynie's confidential secretary and ordinary clerk of the Châtelet. 'The Commission,' writes Ravaisson, 'was composed of the élite of the councillors of state, and all these magistrates have left a high reputation.' The court was called the Chambre Ardente, because in former days tribunals specially constituted to deal with great crimes sat in a chamber hung with black and lit by torches and candles.

The court met for the first time on April 10, 1679, and decided to keep its proceedings secret, so as to withhold details of these practices from the knowledge of the public. The magistrates themselves had no doubt of the efficacy of these dealings with the devil, nor of the formidable composition of the poisons.

The method of procedure was as follows:—

The individuals regarded as suspicious by La Reynie, the examining magistrate, were arrested by royal warrant, that is, by a *lettre de cachet*, which took the place of the modern magistrate's warrant. The first depositions were submitted to the attorney-general, and it was only on his requisition that the officials proceeded to the confrontation of the prisoners, after which the commissaries submitted a detailed report to the court. The attorney presented to them his general conclusions, and the court decided whether the accused person should be 'recommended,' that is, remain a prisoner in virtue of a warrant issued by them. In that case the investigation followed its course. When this was ended, all the documents concerning the accused were read to the judges, the king's attorney delivered his address in favour of acquittal or condemnation, the accused was heard for the last time, and the court pronounced judgment, which was without appeal.

The Chambre Ardente sat in the hall of the Arsenal. From April 10, 1679, the day of its first meeting, to July 21, 1682, when it closed its doors, it held 210 sittings, after having been suspended, for reasons that will be explained later, from October 1, 1680, to May 19, 1681.

The Chambre Ardente deliberated on the fate of 442 accused persons, and ordered the arrest of 367 of these. Of these arrests, 218 were sustained. Thirty-six prisoners were condemned to the extreme penalty, torture ordinary and extraordinary and execution; two of them died a natural death in jail; five were condemned to the galleys; twenty-three were exiled; but the most guilty had accomplices in such high places that their cases were never carried to an end. We must add the prisoners who committed suicide in prison, such as La Dodée, a sorceress aged thirty-five, still very pretty, who was arrested with La Trianon, and cut her throat at Vincennes after her first examination; 'she covered the wound with her chemise, in which the greater part of her blood flowed, and was found dead when her room was opened in the morning to take her her breakfast.'

Among the many cases which came before this court one or two will serve as types.

Madame de Dreux was the wife of a Parlement *maître des requêtes*. She was not yet thirty, and was endowed with much grace and beauty, a delicate and dainty beauty, with infinite charm and distinction. She was so fond of Monsieur de Richelieu, declared La Joly, one of the sorceresses tried by the court, 'that as soon as she knew that Monsieur de Richelieu was even looking at any one else, she thought of doing away with him.' She had further poisoned 'Monsieur Pajot and Monsieur de Varennes and many others,' and, in particular, one of her lovers, to avoid, as she said, the bother and annoyance of a rupture. She had also tried to poison her husband, and to get rid of Madame de Richelieu by sorcery. All these details were widely known in Paris, where society, difficult as it is to believe it, was wonderfully amused by them. The husband was riddled with epigrams, which Madame de Sévigné declares 'divinely diverting.' Madame de Dreux was too pretty, really!—and besides, she was a cousin of two of the judges of the Chambre Ardente; the result was that on April 27, 1680, the judges contented themselves with admonishing her. 'Monsieur de Dreux and her whole family,' writes Madame de Sévigné, 'went to the court to meet her.' Set at liberty, the young woman was fêted and petted by the whole world of fashion. 'There was joy and triumph and kisses from all her family and friends. Monsieur de Richelieu did wonders in this business.' A fact which will appear incredible is, that after she left prison, Madame de Dreux returned to the sorceresses, met La Joly in the Jesuits' church, and asked and obtained from her powders to poison a lady whom Monsieur de Richelieu was 'considering.'

Truth to tell, La Joly was arrested while this was going on, and, as a result of her revelations, a fresh warrant was issued against Madame de Dreux; but she was warned, and escaped. She was proceeded against for contumacy. Her husband and Monsieur de Richelieu were then seen pleading for her in company. On January 23, 1682, Madame de Dreux was condemned to banishment beyond the kingdom, but the king allowed her to remain in France provided she lived in Paris with her husband.

Madame Leféron, who also belonged to judicial society, was less pleasant in appearance. The daughter of a Parlement counsellor, her maiden name was Marguerite Galart. Her husband, president of the first court of *enquêtes*, is represented in the *Tableau du Parlement* of 1661 as 'a good judge, of solid judgment and firm opinion, never changing except on good grounds, unprejudiced, loving rule and order, a good and disinterested man.' He had given proof of independence of character at the time of Fouquet's case, by showing clemency to the superintendent. Madame Leféron found him a bore, avaricious, and further—how can one say it?— insufficient. Yet the fair dame had passed her fiftieth year. But she was madly smitten with one Monsieur de Prade, who on his side was in love with her money. She asked La Voisin for poisons to kill her husband, and de Prade went to her for charms to help him win the heart of his mistress. La Voisin gave them all they wanted: phials to the lady, and to the gallant a mask of virgin wax representing the face of Madame Leféron. This, enclosed in a zinc box, was to be warmed every now and then, which would warm the heart of the lady. De Prade gave La Voisin a note for 20,000 livres—£4000 to-day.

The phials produced their effect, and Leféron died on September 8, 1669. The waxen mask was equally successful, and Madame Leféron married de Prade. On February 20, 1680, as she went to the stake, La Voisin said to Sagot, clerk to the court: 'It is quite true that Madame Leféron came to see me, most joyous at being a widow, and when I asked her if the phial of liquid had taken effect, she said, "Effect or not, he is done for!"' De Prade appeared no less happy. He scoured the city in a brand-new carriage, 'with three or four lackeys behind.' His joy was short. The lady saw that her new husband thought chiefly of getting 'donations' out of her, and the husband soon saw that his wife was trying to poison him in his turn. He fled to the Turks. On April 7, 1680, Madame Leféron was condemned to banishment beyond the borders of the viscounty of Paris and to a fine of 1500 livres, though there were, as Louvois wrote to Louis XIV, thirteen or fourteen witnesses of her crime.

Madame de Dreux and Madame Leféron owed this remarkable indulgence to Madame de Poulaillon. Born Marguerite de Jehan, of a noble Bordeaux family, she had come to Paris when very young to associate with the alchemists, having a passion for the occult sciences. She had married Alexandre de Poulaillon, much older than herself, but very rich. Contemporaries are unanimous in praising the pretty face, the delicate and keen intelligence, and the exquisite distinction of the young lady. Unhappily for herself, she met a certain La Rivière, who had a wonderful talent for getting money out of ladies. As we know, in the seventeenth century, a talent of this sort was not the discreditable thing it is to-day. Her excellent husband, becoming suspicious, drew his purse-strings tight and locked his safes. Madame de Poulaillon had recourse to various expedients. She sold the house furniture, chairs, sofas, 'the big gilded bed upholstered in English watered silk,' the plate, and even the clothes of her husband. He, in a furious temper—we may suppose so, at least—ceased to give his wife even money for her toilet, and bought her dresses and ribbons himself.

In despair, the young woman opened relations with La Vigoureux: she required money for her lover, and the riddance of her husband. With this intent she planned the most audacious strokes. Two or three hired bravoes would do: 'While one held Poulaillon by the throat in his study, the other would throw bags of money out of the window, and she would open the study door herself.' Another time she thought of getting her husband kidnapped alive. She was quite ready herself for the enterprise, but failed to find men to assist her. At last she saw Marie Bosse, who from the first appeared to her more plucky. However, Madame de Poulaillon displayed so furious a haste to get rid of her 'old goodman,' that Marie Bosse, hardened as she was, fairly took fright. She would not give her in one dose the powder necessary for the poisoning, for fear that the lady, by giving it all at once, would create a scandal. The sorceress was prudent enough to begin with the shirt, one of the most horrible of these hags' inventions. The shirts of the husband were washed in arsenic. This left no trace. Whoever put them on was before long attacked by a violent inflammation in the limbs and the lower part of the body. And every one sympathised with the wife whose husband was suffering from a disgraceful malady caused by debauchery! Arsenic was put also into the injections, which in those days were in common use. The contents of a phial poured into the wine or soup hastened the operation.

The negotiations between Madame de Poulaillon and Marie Bosse were carried on in the church of the Carmelites. The young woman gave 4000 livres (£800) for the phial and the preparation for the shirts. Poulaillon was warned by an anonymous letter; moreover, his wife could not obtain the necessary assistance from her servants. Then in her rage she applied to some soldiers, and asked them to wait for her husband at the corner of a road she pointed out to them, where it would be the easiest thing in the world, she said, to do for him. The soldiers took her money and hastened to inform Poulaillon, who now lost all patience, shut his wife up in a convent, and laid an information before the Châtelet. It was at this time that the lady had a writ issued against her by the Chambre Ardente.

As soon as he saw the storm threatening, La Rivière, to whom Madame de Poulaillon had sacrificed everything, fled to Burgundy, where he hid behind the skirts of Madame de Coligny, daughter of the famous Bussy-Rabutin, and widow of the Marquis de Coligny. She fell in love with La Rivière, who, kept informed of the progress of the trial, joked pleasantly with his new flame on the misfortunes of his old mistress. She, though madly in love with the gallant, was shocked. 'If the misfortune of the lady who has so much merit, I hear, and who loves you and has loved you so passionately, no longer touches you, what reason have I to flatter myself I shall keep you always?' This brilliant cavalier, who insisted on being called the Marquis de la Rivière, Lord de Courcy, was really a bastard son of the Abbé de la Rivière, Bishop of Langres.

Madame de Poulaillon was finally examined on June 5, 1679. The attorney-general had demanded the penalty of torture and death on the Place de Grève; but the memory of the edifying and touching end of Madame de Brinvilliers was still strong in the minds of the judges, and had almost stricken them with remorse. Madame de Poulaillon displayed before her judges even more grace, more submission to the hand of God, more sweet and tranquil resignation. So strongly were these men of law moved, that they could not bring themselves to order the severing of that charming head. 'This lady, who had infinite spirit,' notes Sagot the clerk, 'cared little about death, and though she did not expect to escape, showed during her whole examination an extraordinary presence of mind, which won the judges' admiration and pity.' La Reynie writes that the judges were touched 'by her spirit, and by the grace with which at the last she explained her unhappiness and her crime.' 'The commissioners,' says Sagot, 'remained in deliberation for four whole hours, all of them, especially those who had some interest in these ladies, being prepared for anything which might serve, if not for the discharge of Madame de Poulaillon, at any rate for the mitigation of the facts they could not dispute, in so far as that could be done without a manifest miscarriage of justice. Monsieur de Fieubet was the one who dilated most on this view, employing all the power of his natural eloquence; and he it was who saved the life of Madame de Poulaillon, having brought round to his way of thinking three of the six judges who had previously decided for death. This was a precedent fortunate for Mesdames de Dreux and Leféron and other prisoners, and in fact it was through this that the court lost credit.'

'The great difficulty,' adds La Reynie, 'was afterwards to console Madame de Poulaillon when she found that she was only condemned to exile instead of the death she had herself pronounced in presence of the judges, after having declared the joy she had in thus expiating her crime, and at the same time winning deliverance from all her other woes.' On the demand of the young lady herself, her punishment was increased by royal warrant to detention with the Penitents at Angers. Meanwhile La Rivière, after making Madame de Coligny a mother, married her without a trace of compunction. True, shortly afterwards, Bussy-Rabutin and his daughter, undeceived about the man, endeavoured to dissolve the union; but the gay spark resisted, and Madame de la Rivière was forced to pension him off at a very high figure before he would agree to desert her.

The best society applauded the acquittal of Madame de Poulaillon, while the middle classes murmured, with so much the more reason that soon afterwards a certain widow lady named Brunet was condemned with the greatest harshness, though no more guilty than Mesdames de Poulaillon, de Dreux, and Leféron.

She had been the wife of a wholesale tradesman in the city. Monsieur and Madame Brunet entertained very largely, for they provided excellent music. The fashionable flutist, Philibert Rébillé, musician to the king, was constantly to be heard there. Brunet worshipped the flutist for his delightful skill, and Madame Brunet for his charming person. As the excellent people kept a good table, and the wife was charming, the artiste responded with great enthusiasm to this double passion. It was perfect bliss, which might have lasted for a long time to the melodious sounds of the flute, if Brunet, with the idea of permanently attaching to himself so pleasant a musician, had not taken it into his head to offer him his daughter with a handsome dowry, and if Philibert, delighted with the ducats and the daughter, had not accepted them with alacrity. Madame Brunet uttered a cry of horror! Philibert explained to her that he had consulted apostolic notaries, and that for a consideration it would be possible to obtain canonical letters which would set things right; and festivities were got up for the betrothal. In desperation Madame Brunet confided in La Voisin: 'If she had to do penance for ten years, it was necessary that God should carry off Brunet, her husband, for she could not abide to see Philibert, whom she loved passionately, in the arms of her daughter.' She even took her lover to the sorceress. Philibert deposed at the trial that, under pretext of showing him a garden, Madame Brunet took him to see a woman who proceeded to look at his hand: 'I know not who she is, for the woman was so drunk that she could not say a word.' La Voisin, on being questioned, related the proceedings of Madame Brunet, adding: 'There are other details which I would not tell for anything in the world, I would rather have a dagger thrust into my heart: that is kept for confessors, not for judges.' François Ravaisson, in publishing this dramatic declaration, thus comments on it: 'These details were imparted by La Voisin to La Reynie later; they did honour to Philibert's disposition. The details given by the judges brought this flute-player into the height of fashion, and ladies of the court and the city scrambled for him when he came out of prison.'

Meanwhile, Marie Bosse undertook the operation, for 2000 livres—£400 to-day.

Brunet was poisoned in 1673, and Philibert married the widow.

'My friends advised me,' he declared naïvely before the judges, 'to wed the mother rather than the daughter, which I did, under the good pleasure of the king, who signed the contract.'

The flute-player's wife was condemned on May 15, 1679. She begged in vain to be allowed to see husband and children for the last time. Her hand was cut off while she was still alive, then she was hanged, and her body cast into the fire. Louis XIV, who was fond of his flutist, advised him to leave France if he was conscious of guilt. But Philibert was a man of mettle. He went like a gentleman and gave himself up as a prisoner at Vincennes. He was acquitted on April 7, 1680.

Louis XIV and the Poison Affair

Meanwhile the Chambre Ardente was extending its prosecutions over an ever-widening circle and into higher and higher ranks of society, and by degrees a singular disquietude awoke, an astonishing uneasiness: it was no longer the poisoners whom people dreaded, but the magistrates. People talked about a lady of the highest rank who was declaring everywhere that the judges and all their proceedings ought to be burnt. La Reynie asked for the protection of an escort when he went to Vincennes, where the principal accused persons were. Madame de Sévigné, speaking of the great lieutenant of police, wrote: 'His life is a proof that there are no poisoners now.' On February 4, 1680, Louvois wrote to the president of the court:—

'His Majesty, having been informed of what was said in Paris in regard to the decrees issued a few days ago by the Chamber, has commanded me to acquaint you with His Majesty's desire that you should assure the judges of his protection, and let them understand that he expects them to continue dispensing justice with firmness.'

Louis sent for Boucherat, the president, the two examining commissioners, La Reynie and Bezons, and the attorney-general, and they went out to Versailles. 'On rising from dinner,' writes La Reynie, 'His Majesty recommended us to do justice and our duty, in extremely strong and precise terms, indicating to us that he desired, on behalf of the public weal, that we should penetrate as deeply as possible into the terrible traffic in poisons, so as to cut its root if this were possible; he commanded us to do strict justice, without distinction of person, rank, or sex; and this His Majesty told us in clear and vigorous terms.'

The determination so vigorously expressed by the king filled La Reynie with confidence and zeal; it encouraged him in the accomplishment of the arduous task imposed on him. And such courage was necessary: what frightful revelations he heard! Was it due to these revelations that, suddenly, the intentions of the court of Versailles underwent modification? La Voisin had just been condemned to suffer torture. She was subjected to it, but only as a matter of form. 'La Voisin was not tortured at all,' writes La Reynie in indignation, 'and this means not having been applied, has naturally produced no effect.' It was feared that the sorceress, whose discretion had been so remarkable hitherto, might say too much in the agony of torture, and, independently of La Reynie, the torturers had received their orders. The judges had also received independent orders, and their reluctance to interrogate the accused woman was such that, at the moment of her execution, La Voisin, struck with remorse, conceived it her duty to confess spontaneously before being handed over to the confessor: 'She felt obliged to say, to ease her conscience, that a large number of persons of all ranks and conditions had applied to her for means to procure the death of many persons, and that debauchery was the chief motive of all these crimes.'

But after the execution of La Voisin, the examinations of her partner Lesage, of her accomplice the Abbé Guibourg, and of her daughter, Marguerite Monvoisin, were proceeded with. On August 2, 1680, Louis XIV wrote from Lille to La Reynie:—

'Having seen the declaration made on the 12th of last month by Marguerite Monvoisin, prisoner at my castle of Vincennes, I write you this letter to inform you of my intention that you should devote all possible care to elucidate the facts contained in the said declaration—that you should take care to have written down in separate reports the examinations, confrontations, and everything concerning the inquiry that may be made of the said declaration, and that meanwhile you defer reporting to my royal Chamber sitting at the Arsenal the depositions of Romani and Bertrand.'

Romani and Bertrand were two prisoners with whom we shall have a good deal to do by and by.

Thus Louis XIV gave orders for the declarations of the girl Monvoisin, and those of Romani and Bertrand, to be detached from the documents submitted to the court. On the other hand, Louvois had had the imprudence to promise Lesage his life if he revealed all he knew. Lesage related most horrible things. Word then went round not to listen to any more; he was a liar. But on September 30 and October 1, 1680, these narratives were confirmed in the most precise manner by the sorceress Françoise Filastre while under torture. The declarations of Filastre struck on the ears of Louis XIV like a clap of thunder. In the registers of the royal council we read as follows:—

'The king, having had shown to him the official report of the torture of Françoise Filastre, being unwilling to permit, for good and just considerations important to his service, that certain facts should be inserted in the copies made for the convenience of the Court of the Arsenal, His Majesty in Council has commanded that the minutes and originals of the said proceedings be laid before the chancellor by the clerk to the commission, and that the said clerk draw up in his presence a summary of the said proceedings, in which the said facts shall not be inserted. Given by His Majesty in Council held at Versailles, May 14, 1681.

(Signed) LE TELLIER.'

Thus the king for the second time intervened, and withdrew from the court certain documents containing new declarations. He saw now, moreover, that these were in accordance with the truth, and that if the examinations were continued, it would be impossible to prevent them from being divulged. On October 1, 1680, the sittings of the court were suspended.

The documents which the king had thus caused to be separated from the rest were locked and sealed up in a casket, which was deposited with Sagot, the clerk, who lived in the Rue Quincampoix. When Sagot died, on October 10, 1680, the casket was removed to Rue Sainte-Croix-de-la-Bretonnerie, to the house of his successor in the clerkship to the Châtelet and the Chambre Ardente, Nicolas Gaudion. On July 13, 1709, the casket was taken to the king's private room, where, in the presence of Chancellor Pontchartrain, Louis XIV burnt the papers in his grate: 'His Majesty in Council, after having looked through and examined the minutes and proceedings laid before him by the chancellor, and having had them burnt in his presence, commanded that Gaudion should then be wholly and formally discharged of the same.'

Louis XIV had just suffered a cruel blow, not only in his deepest affections, but in his dignity as sovereign, by the declarations of obscure and infamous criminals made before the Chambre Ardente. The very throne of France was befouled by them. Colbert and Louvois were for a moment in dire alarm. The all-powerful monarch, aided by his two great ministers, believed that he had buried in unfathomable darkness the terrible story of his shame and grief. But one flame had not been extinguished. It had not been noticed. But it has continued to burn, and grown larger, and thrown its blaze widely around. It is in the full daylight glare that the facts are about to appear before our eyes.

II. MADAME DE MONTESPAN

The Marquise Françoise Athénais de Montespan was born in 1641 at the castle of Tonnay-Charente, the daughter of Gabriel de Rochechouart, Duke de Mortmart, lord of Vivonne, and of Diane de Granseigne, daughter of Jean de Marsillac. She was called Mademoiselle de Tonnay-Charente until her marriage. 'Her mother,' says Madame de Caylus, 'was anxious to imbue her with principles of sound piety.' The piety of Mademoiselle de Tonnay-Charente was violent and inflammatory. Appointed in 1660 maid of honour to the queen, 'she gave her an extraordinary opinion of her virtue by taking communion every day.' In 1679, when she had been for several years the king's mistress, she much astonished the Princess d'Harcourt by sending her on January 1, as a new year's gift, a hair-shirt, a scourge, and a prayer-book adorned with diamonds.

Mademoiselle de Tonnay-Charente married, on January 28, 1663, a noble of her own province, L. H. de Pardaillan, Marquis de Montespan, who was a year younger than herself. If she ever loved him, it was not for long. As a lady-in-waiting to the queen, she was fascinated by the magnificence surrounding Louise de la Vallière, the favourite of Louis, who had become, in spite of her reserve and her timid and gentle bearing, the object of intense and widespread jealousy, hatred, and wrath. Madame de Montespan especially displayed her spiteful envy in malicious gibes and insulting irony. Everybody knows it was not long before she replaced her.

Louise de la Vallière had kept in the shade, shunning publicity and honours; Madame de Montespan in her pride wished to dazzle all eyes. 'Thunderous and triumphant' is Madame de Sévigné's description of her in her radiant glory at Versailles. She draws elsewhere a picture of the court in which the king's favourite shone: 'At three o'clock the king and queen, with Monsieur, Madame, Mademoiselle, all the princes and princesses, Madame de Montespan, all her suite, all the courtiers and ladies, in a word, all that is known as the court of France, were found in these handsome apartments of the king. They are divinely furnished, everything is magnificent. Madame de

Montespan was dressed in *point de France*, her hair done in a thousand curls, two hanging from her temples very low upon her cheeks; black ribbons on her head, with her pearls as *maréchale* of the Hospital, and embellished with earrings and pendants; in a word, a triumph of beauty that threw the ambassadors into admiring wonder. She knew that people were complaining how she prevented all France from seeing the king; she has restored him to us, as you see, and you would not believe what joy it has given everybody, and what beauty it has given the court.'

'Her beauty is marvellous,' writes Madame de Sévigné on another day, 'and her get-up is as wonderful as her beauty, and her gaiety as her get-up.' Greater still was the renown of her wit. 'She was always the best of company,' says Saint-Simon, 'with graces which palliated her high and mighty airs, and were indeed suited to them. It was impossible to have more wit, more fine polish, more striking expressions, eloquence, natural propriety, which gave her, as it were, an individual style of talk, but delicious, and which by force of habit was so communicable that her nieces and the persons constantly about her, her women, and those who, without being her servants, had been brought up along with her, all caught the style, which is recognisable to-day among the few survivors.'

She surrounded herself with a brilliant luxury. Here is one of her dresses as described by Madame de Sévigné: 'Gold upon gold, gold embroideries, gold edgings, and, over all, gold crimpings, sewed with one sort of gold blended with another sort, which makes up the divinest stuff imaginable: it was the fairies who made this masterpiece in secret.'

In her estates at Clagny, with their immense park, a second Versailles was to be seen alongside Versailles itself. The king had first had built there for his mistress a bijou residence—a country villa. 'She said that that might do for an opera girl.' The house was pulled down and the château erected, after the plans of Mansard. At Versailles the favourite had twenty rooms on the first floor; the queen occupied eleven rooms on the second. Dangeau notes that Madame de Montespan's train was borne by the Maréchale de Noailles; the queen's was carried by a simple page.

The influence of the young favourite spelled fortune, hope, and honour to ministers, courtiers, and generals. Her father became governor of Paris, her brother a marshal of France. In her drawing-room, frequented by all the most distinguished persons in rank and literature, a quite unique style of wit came into existence, which her contemporaries often refer to—a wit at once choice and subtle, natural and pleasant. It must be added that, by a wonderful coincidence, her reign, which lasted thirteen years, exactly corresponded with the zenith of the age of Louis XIV.

Madame de Montespan used to go about escorted by royal bodyguards. As she journeyed throughout the whole length and breadth of France, governors and lord-lieutenants offered her their homage in great ceremony, and cities sent deputations to her. She passed through the provinces in a six-horse coach, followed by another coach also drawn by six horses, in which sat six ladies of her suite, and then came the baggage-wagons and six mules and a dozen cavaliers. It is like a fairy tale from Perrault.

She had by Louis XIV seven children, whom the Parlement was to legitimatise and declare royal children of France. The oldest, the Duke de Maine, received the principality of Dombes and the county of Eu; in 1675, when five years old, he was appointed to the infantry regiment of Marshal Turenne; in 1682, the king gave him the governorship of Languedoc; on September 15, 1688, the office of general of the galleys and the lieutenant-generalship of the Levant. The elder of the daughters, Mademoiselle de Nantes, married the Duke de Bourbon; the second, Mademoiselle de Blois, made a still more brilliant match. 'The king,' says Saint-Simon, 'determined to marry Mademoiselle de Blois to the Duke de Chartres; this was the king's only nephew, and far higher than the princes of the blood.'

Madame Palatine[9] said of the Marquise de Montespan: 'She is more ambitious than dissipated.' There is justice in the saying. She had an immeasurable pride. Mademoiselle de la Vallière loved the king as a mistress, Madame de Maintenon as a governess, Madame de Montespan as a tyrant.

It was in 1666 that historians note the first signs of Madame de Montespan's ambition. She was then aspiring to the king's love, and it is precisely at this time that La Reynie, in commenting on the proceedings of the Chambre Ardente, places her first visits to the sorceresses.

Marguerite Monvoisin, La Voisin's daughter, spoke thus before the judges: 'Every time that anything fresh happened to Madame de Montespan, or she feared any diminution in the favour of the king, she told my mother, so that she might provide a remedy; and my mother at once had recourse to priests whom she got to say masses, and gave my mother powders to be given to the king.' La Voisin's daughter explained that these powders were for love, composed now in one way, now in another, according to the various formulae of witchcraft. Among the ingredients were cantharides, the dust of dried moles, blood of bats, and other vile substances. Of these a paste was made, which was placed under the chalice during the sacrifice of the mass, and blessed by the priest at the moment of the offertory. Louis XIV swallowed this compound mixed with his food.

'My mother,' said the girl, 'several times took to Madame de Montespan at Saint-Germain, Versailles, and Clagny, these love-powders to give to the king—some which had passed under the chalice and others which had not; my mother sent some to Madame de Montespan by the hand of the demoiselle Desœillets (one of her waiting-maids), and I myself gave her some in the church of the Petits Pères, and another time on the road to St. Cloud.'

The depositions of Marguerite Monvoisin are important. She had never been mixed up with her mother's sorceries, but she had known about them. La Reynie observes that her declarations exhibit 'a certain air of ingenuousness, or else, if they are false, every one is mightily deceived.' He adds that 'she mentions so many circumstances and so many different transactions which are not self-contradictory, that it is morally impossible for them to have been invented, in addition to which she is not clever enough to invent and to follow up what she has invented. Several of these facts are proved genuine; she mentions living people.' The examining judge says further, that the very denials of the sorceresses accused by Marguerite of complicity with Madame de Montespan, their embarrassment, their contradictions, their refusal to answer when they were conscious of being hard pressed, confirm her testimony.

When Marguerite Monvoisin made her depositions, her mother had been dead for several months. In the examination of July 12, 1680, we read:—

'Why did you not sooner give information of these evil designs against the person of the king?'

'I could not tell what I had heard without ruining my mother; I did not believe myself obliged to tell; I asked advice of no one, and have declared all I know on the matter.'

'Did you not know you were bound to tell, and that it would be a great crime to hide anything concerning this matter?'

'I knew well enough the importance of the things I have stated; I knew it before I told them, and was sure of it after I had done so; and I knew there was nothing but was of great importance.'

'Did you know it would be a great crime to make the slightest addition to the facts which you have declared?'

'Yes, and those of whom I have spoken can tell you a good deal; I think I have diminished rather than increased; I had no other idea but to state the truth, having nothing more to fear in regard to my mother; if I remember any other circumstance, or if any is recalled to my memory, I will confess the truth.'

Several writers have thought that the sorceresses compromised the greatest names in France before the judges in the hope of saving their lives, by connecting themselves with personages so high in station that no one would dare to lift a hand against them. Quite the contrary. We see La Voisin concealing, up to the very moment of her execution, her relations with the king's mistress, for her greatest fear was that the horrible punishment meted out to regicides might be applied to her. In an expansive moment, she said to her guards at Vincennes: 'I fear, more than anything else that I am asked about, a certain journey to court.' We shall have much to do presently with this journey the sorceress made to court on behalf of Madame de Montespan. It was at the last moment, after hearing her death-sentence, against which there was no appeal, that Françoise Filastre made her startling depositions of September 30 and October 1, 1680, as the result of which Louis XIV, in terror, caused the sittings of the Chambre Ardente to be suspended.

The statements of Marguerite Monvoisin were confirmed in detail by those of the Abbé Guibourg, with whom she had no means of communicating after her arrest. Thus, as La Reynie says, they were proved 'according to the rules of justice.'

To-day, history furnishes still further proofs. We have just heard the daughter of La Voisin: 'Every time anything fresh happened to Madame de Montespan, or she feared some diminution in the favour of the king, she told my mother.' Now, if we follow in the correspondence of Madame de Sévigné and the court chronicles the checkered story of the relations between Madame de Montespan and the king from 1667 to 1680, and compare it further with the depositions made before the Chambre Ardente, we find a precise confirmation of the declarations of Marguerite Monvoisin. It was several times observed by La Reynie that 'the time mentioned by the accused is of consequence to Madame de Montespan.'

How, and by whom, was the haughty favourite led to the haunts of the witches? Historians have put forth many hypotheses on this subject. They were not acquainted with the declaration of La Chaboissière, the valet of Vanens, whom we have already mentioned: 'that the chevalier de Vanens deserved to be drawn and quartered for the counsel he had given to Madame de Montespan.' La Chaboissière had scarcely let this confession escape him than he wished in great agitation to retract it, and begged that the words might not be written down in the report of his examination. La Reynie disentangled this confession from the chaos of official documents, and sharply underlined it as the starting-point of the drama.

The relations between the favourite and the sorceresses began, then, at the very time when her dawning love for the king was noticed. In 1667 we find her in Rue de la Tannerie, in the company of the magician Lesage and the Abbé Mariette, priest of St. Séverin. The latter belonged to a good Parisian family; he was tall and well made, with a very pale complexion and black hair. At one end of a little room an altar was erected: Mariette, in sacerdotal vestments, uttered incantations, Lesage sang the *Veni Creator*, then Mariette read a gospel on the head of Madame de Montespan, who knelt before him and recited exorcisms against Louise de la Vallière. She added—the very words are found in one of Lesage's declarations—'I ask for the affection of the king and of the Dauphin, that it may be continued, that the queen may be barren, that the king leave her bed and table for me, that I obtain from him all that I ask for myself and my relatives; that my servants and domestics may be pleasing to him; that, beloved and respected by great nobles, I may be called to the councils of the king and know what passes there; and that, this affection being redoubled on what has existed in the past, the king may leave La Vallière and look no more upon her; and that, the queen being repudiated, I may espouse the king.'

On another occasion, in the church of St. Severin, the Abbé Mariette, in the presence of Madame de Montespan, recited charms over the hearts of two pigeons which had been consecrated in the names of Louis XIV and Louise de la Vallière during the sacrifice of the mass.

Early in the year 1668, Mariette and Lesage had the audacity to proceed to Saint-Germain, the headquarters of the court, and in the very château itself, in the portion occupied by Madame de Thianges, Madame de Montespan's sister, they resumed their sorceries. Aromatic fumigations filled the room with a bluish vapour, with which was mingled the pungent scent of incense. Madame de Montespan formulated the incantation. 'This,' declared Lesage, 'was to obtain the favour of the king, and to cause Mademoiselle de la Vallière's death.' Mariette said it was merely to get her sent away. Now it happened that, not long after these proceedings, in that very year 1668, Madame de Montespan realised her dream and was taken to the king's heart. The star of La Vallière rapidly paled. In 1669 Madame de Montespan was brought to bed of the first of the seven children she gave to Louis. If she had ever doubted the efficacy of these dealings with the devil, confidence would have dated from that day.

An incident, which might have had terrible consequences, ruffled this happiness so long desired. Mariette and Lesage owed to La Voisin the lucrative connection with Madame de Montespan. But they showed base ingratitude, and proceeded to perform incantations for the marquise, no longer with the assistance of La Voisin, but with that of a rival sorceress, La Duverger. La Voisin was indignant, and as La Reynie says, 'made a to-do about it. The matter became known, and the king, having learnt that these people were accustomed to perform impious and sacrilegious rites, ordered the arrest of Mariette and Dubuisson (the name taken by Lesage at this period), and they were sent to the Bastille in March 1668.' From the Bastille they were brought before the Châtelet on the charge of sorcery. The court chroniclers, though ignorant of her reasons for so doing, note that Madame de Montespan at this time suddenly left Paris. But Mariette and Lesage had too much interest in holding their tongues to inform against her. 'Besides,' writes La Reynie, 'the first judge who heard the case being a cousin-german of Mariette through his wife, La Voisin being at large on the credit of interested persons with whom she had dealings, and these wretched practices being then unknown, investigation was not carried very far. It was solely a question of seeing how the matter could be dealt with in such a way as to save Mariette on account of his family.' The little that could not be concealed brought Lesage condemnation to the galleys and Mariette banishment. The king increased the sentence of the latter to imprisonment; but the prisoner escaped from St. Lazare, where he had been confined. As to Lesage, La Voisin, thanks to her connections, was not long in getting him set at liberty. In a memorandum addressed to Louvois, La Reynie exhibits the conclusions to be drawn from the trial of 1668. After very appositely calling attention to the fact that the statements of the accused were the less suspicious because, dating from a period when as yet there could be no question of the scarcely dawning relations between Louis and Madame de Montespan, the lieutenant of police says that Mariette and Lesage could only have known of those relations through Madame de Montespan herself, and adds: 'It appears from the trial of Lesage and Mariette in 1668, that Madame de Montespan had been dealing with La Voisin at any rate since 1667, and that about that time she was by her introduced to Lesage and Mariette; that Mariette, in his room and in the presence of Lesage, used to read the Gospels over the head of Madame de Montespan.

'So early as that, then, a scheme was on foot.

'When I questioned the two surviving accomplices on the matter, they said, separately, that this scheme was to secure the favour of the king; that for that purpose La Voisin then gave some powders which were placed under the chalice given to Madame de Montespan, and that she recited an incantation in which her own name and the king's occurred; that she performed other ceremonies at Saint-Germain; that she had masses said on the hearts of pigeons at St. Séverin, and other impious and sacrilegious rites performed in Mariette's room, for this purpose, and as the one says, to slay, the other merely to get rid of, Madame de la Vallière.' (These enchantments to procure the death of Mademoiselle de la Vallière were made upon human bones.)

'Lesage and Mariette said nothing about it until the former, urged by explicit commands to tell the truth, and Mariette, impelled by the facts themselves to reveal them, both, separately, established these facts.'

La Reynie observes further that Lesage and Mariette mentioned certain details, afterwards proved to be accurate, of which they could have got information from Madame de Montespan alone.

We have already mentioned the reasons why the declarations of Marguerite Monvoisin inspired confidence; the corresponding depositions of Lesage deserve equal attention. On October 8, 1679, Louvois wrote to Louis *XIV*: 'Monsieur de la Reynie showed me his conviction that, if I spoke to Lesage, he would in the end make up his mind to tell me all he knew, and he believed this to be the more important because this man has not up to the present been convicted himself of poisoning any one, but has a perfect knowledge of all the poisonings effected in Paris for the last seven or eight years. I went yesterday to Vincennes, and spoke to him in the way Monsieur de la Reynie desired, giving him to hope that your Majesty would pardon him provided he made the declarations necessary for bringing to the knowledge of justice all that has happened in regard to the poisons. He promised to do so, and told me that he was much surprised at my urging him to tell all he knew.' In a letter of October 11, 1679, Louvois renewed his pressure on Lesage to induce him to speak fully and in entire frankness. The magician hesitated, tried to dissimulate, repeating to all who urged him how vastly he was astonished at their persistence; but this reluctance only stimulated the ardour of La Reynie. He returned to the charge; like Louvois, he gave hints of a royal pardon. At last Lesage spoke. His principal declarations were written among the papers which Louis had burnt in the fireplace of his study, as we have said; hence we no longer possess them in their entirety; but from the notes left by La Reynie, as well as from the fragments of the magisterial examination which were preserved and will be found in part reproduced below, we know that the revelations of Lesage entirely confirmed those of Marguerite Monvoisin.

The scandal of the amours of Louis XIV was only the more intense because the young Marquis de Montespan was by no means a complaisant husband, a singular fact at that period and in that society. 'He was an extravagant and extraordinary man,' says Mademoiselle de Montpensier, 'who complained to everybody of the friendship of the king for his wife.' There were scenes between the spouses, and he struck her. He provoked scenes with the king. 'When Montespan went to Saint-Germain sermonising thus, Madame de Montespan was in despair. He used to come to see me very often,' says Mademoiselle de Montpensier; 'he is a relative of mine, and I scolded him. He came one evening and repeated to me an harangue he had delivered to the king, in which he quoted innumerable passages of Scripture, about David, for instance, and finally used strong terms to induce him to give back his wife and fear the judgment of God. I said to him, "You are mad!" I was at Saint-Germain next day and said to Madame de Montespan: "I have seen your husband in Paris, and he is madder than ever; I sharply scolded him and told him that if he didn't hold his tongue he would deserve to be locked up." She said to me: "He is here telling his tales at court; I am ashamed to see that my parrot and he are amusing the mob."'

Louis XIV was naturally irritated by the attitude of this surprising husband. Almighty as he was, he resorted to the tricks and subterfuges of a vulgar lover. His anxiety was redoubled when his mistress became a mother. The king was very fond of his children, particularly those he had by Madame de Montespan. In the eyes of the law these children belonged to the husband; and Louis trembled with fear lest Montespan, out of vengeance or irony, should come and take from him his son and daughter.

Montespan found a supporter in his uncle the Archbishop of Sens. 'When the king's passion was known,' says the Abbé Boileau, brother of the poet, 'the archbishop sentenced to public penance a woman of the town who lived as the marchioness, his niece, was living, in open concubinage, and he caused the publication in his diocese of the old canons against the violation of the religious law.' The diocese of Sens included Fontainebleau, where the court was then held. Madame de Montespan was compelled to take her departure in confusion. She felt that it was she who was being pointed at. She dared not return into the jurisdiction of the archbishop until after the prelate's death in 1674.

When the Marquis understood that his efforts were vain, and that from the height of his throne Louis would reply only with *lettres de cachet*, he put on mourning, clothed all his household in black, and drove to the court in a coach draped in black, to take leave in great ceremony of his relatives, friends, and acquaintances. On that day the husband in his costume of black was not the butt of ridicule; jests were silenced, and the king on the throne was scorned and despised. A man of genius lent the monarch his aid. Molière wrote his *Amphitryon*. The play was represented in this year 1668, and the mockers resumed their places in the royal camp.

'Un partage avec Jupiter
N'a rien du tout qui déshonore.'[10]

Viscounts and marquises on gilded benches applauded the taunt and punctuated the cruel railleries with bursts of laughter. Yet the king was injured, especially in the opinion of the Parisian middle class. He was conscious of it; and one day said himself to his mistress that if she had left house, children, and husband to follow him, he had neglected the care of his reputation, which was much blighted through his having loved a woman whom he had such good reasons for not regarding as he had done.

Montespan set out for his country seat. Some men of the company he commanded fell a-quarrelling with the under-bailiff of Perpignan; the fact was of no importance, but it came to the knowledge of the ministers, and Louvois wrote at once to the Lord Lieutenant: 'September 21, 1669. I cannot express my surprise that a thing of the nature of that which Monsieur de Montespan has done should have passed without my learning of it. I send you a despatch from the king for the supreme council of Roussillon, in which His Majesty commands the council to hold an inquiry. In whatever manner you may employ it, it must not be forgotten, whether in the informations of the sub-bailiff of Perpignan or in that about the disorders that occurred at Illes, to implicate the commander of the company (Montespan) and the largest possible number of cavaliers, so that they may take fright and the majority desert, especially the commander; after which it would not be a difficult matter to bring about the ruin of the company. If you have the names of the cavaliers who insulted the sub-bailiff, they must be arrested at once, to make an example of them, and so that you may have, from their depositions at the time of their execution, more proof against the captain—to try in some way or other to implicate him in the informations, so that he may be cashiered with an appearance of justice. If you could manage that he is accused sufficiently for the supreme council to have grounds for pronouncing some condemnation on him, it would be a very good thing; you will guess the reasons well enough, however little you may be informed of what is going on in this part of the world.' The cynicism of Louis and his minister passes all bounds. Montespan had to flee for refuge to Spain; but from that day Louis' position in regard to the injured husband, so far from improving, became sensibly worse. Abroad, Montespan could more boldly and independently press his claims on the children of the king, and provoke a scandal in the eyes of all Europe.

Louis got a demand for separation *a mensa et thoro*, formulated by Madame de Montespan, brought before the Châtelet. Notwithstanding the pressure exerted by king and ministers, who bullied the judges, the matter remained in suspense. The judges could not bring themselves to commit the iniquity demanded of them. They gave way at last, partly under pressure from the First President de Novion, who had been won by a promise of the

Great Seal. The separation was declared on July 7, 1674, by Procureur-Général Achille de Harlay, assisted by six judges. The judgment adduced the wasting of the property of the commonalty by the Marquis de Montespan, the domestic discord between the marquis and his wife, and the ill-treatment of which the marchioness complained on the part of her husband. This decree pronounced against Montespan was a monstrous proceeding. After having dishonoured his crown, Louis dishonoured justice; but there was a higher justice which, as we shall see, he was not to escape.

The decree of July 7, 1674, did not assure the king peace of mind. In 1678 Montespan had to return for a short time to Paris on account of a lawsuit. Louis XIV wrote to Colbert (June 15): 'I understand that Montespan is indulging in indiscreet talk; he is a madman whom you will do me the pleasure to have closely watched; and so that he may have no pretext for remaining in Paris, see Novion so that the Parlement may hurry. I know that Montespan has threatened to see his wife, and that he is capable of it, and that the consequences might be formidable (the question of the children again); I rely on you to prevent him speaking. Do not forget the details of this matter, and especially see to it that he leaves Paris at the earliest moment.' Such were the jobs to which the Colberts and the Louvois had to stoop; but such also were the annoyances and troubles beneath which Louis bent his brow—a brow already reddened with shame, and soon to be furrowed with grief.

Louis XIV loved his mistresses, not for their own sakes, but for his. The new passion lasted three years. Perhaps some one will say that that is a good while. In 1672, jealousy, which perpetually ravaged the proud soul of Madame de Montespan, burst out in storms of which Madame de Sévigné speaks thus: 'She is in inexpressible rages; she has seen no one for a fortnight; she writes from morning till night, and when she goes to bed tears it all up. Her state makes me quite sorry. No one pities her, though she has done good turns to many people.' Madame de Montespan returned to La Voisin; and it is not without emotion that we see this wonderful woman, with her matchless grace and her superior intelligence, after having stepped into crime, sinking into it lower and lower. From the hands of the Abbé Mariette, who recited the Gospels over her head and made incantations on the hearts of pigeons, she comes into those of the Abbé Guibourg, who said the black mass.

Guibourg claimed to be an illegitimate member of the family of Montmorency. He was seventy years old; his complexion was that of a confirmed toper. He had a horrible squint. In these monstrous ceremonies he cut the throats of his own children by his mistress, a fat ruddy wench named Chanfrain.

To obtain the desired result from the black mass, it was necessary that it should be celebrated three times in succession. The three masses were said in 1673, at intervals of a fortnight or three weeks—the first in the chapel of the Château of Villebousin, in the village of Mesnil, near Montlhéry. Mademoiselle Desœillets, the maid of Madame de Montespan, was intimately connected with Leroy, governor of the pages of the Petite Ecurie, who owned a house at Mesnil. Guibourg had lived in the château as almoner of the Montgommerys. It has been described by M. J. Lair: 'A building of the fourteenth century, and well chosen for sinister incantations, the château, situated half a league from the road from Paris to Orleans, was surrounded by deep moats, filled with running water.' Leroy betook himself to St. Denis, where he saw the Abbé Guibourg. He promised fifty pistoles, that is, about £20, and a living worth 2000 livres. At the day fixed there met at Villebousin Madame de Montespan, the Abbé Guibourg, Leroy, 'a tall person' who was certainly Mademoiselle Desœillets, and a person of name unknown who is said to have been a retainer of the Archbishop of Sens. In the chapel of the chateau the priest said mass on the bare body of the favourite as she lay across the altar. At the consecration, he recited his incantation, the words of which he gave later to the commissaries of the Chambre Ardente: 'Ashtaroth, Asmodeus, Princes of Affection, I conjure you to accept the sacrifice I present to you of this child for the things I ask of you, which are that the affection of the king and my lord the dauphin for me may be continued; and that, honoured by the princes and princesses of the court, nothing be denied me of all that I shall ask the king, as well for my relatives as my servitors.' 'Guibourg had bought for a crown (12s. 6d. to-day) the child who was sacrificed at this mass,' writes La Reynie, 'and who was offered to him by a fine girl; and having drawn blood from the child, whom he stabbed in the throat with a penknife, he poured it into the chalice, after which the child was taken away and carried to another place.'

The details of the mass at Mesnil were revealed by Guibourg, and further confirmed by the deposition of La Chanfrain, his mistress.

The second mass on the body of Madame de Montespan took place a fortnight or three weeks after the first, at St. Denis, in a tumbledown hut. The third took place in a house at Paris, whither Guibourg was conducted blindfold, and from which he was brought back in the same way as far as the arcade of the Hôtel de Ville.

At this time the journal of the health of the king, drawn up by D'Aquin, the chief physician, states that Louis suffered from violent headaches. Towards the end of this year, 1673, he was attacked by dizziness of such a kind that at times his sight became clouded and he felt on the point of collapse. 'Is it rash,' observes Monsieur Loiseleur very justly, 'to see in these headaches and faintnesses the effect of powders provided by La

Voisin?' The hypothesis of Monsieur Loiseleur will be sustained in detail by a declaration of the magician Lesage which will be found below.

It remains to inquire how Madame de Montespan contrived to get the powders prepared by the sorceress into the food of the king, surrounded as he was by officers of the buttery. Two revelations, both of November 8, 1680, made, the first by Lemaire, locked up at Vincennes with the Abbé Guibourg, the second by Lesage, will give the indication we desire.

We read in the notes La Reynie took for his personal guidance by way of memoranda: 'November 8, 1680, Lemaire asked to speak to me; told me that being in the same room with Guibourg and another man, Guibourg told them such strange things, especially in regard to Madame de Montespan, that he does not know what to make of it, and that if there was any officer who ought to be suspected, it would be Duchesne, the butler; that Duchesne was a footman in the house of Madame d'Aubray, that he has since served Monsieur Bontemps, and then Madame de Montespan, who was very kind to him, and made him officer of the buttery, and that he is always at Madame de Montespan's service.' Further: 'From the last examinations of Lesage, and that of November 8 particularly, it appears that Gilot, also an officer of the buttery, was involved in the impious trade in 1668, and that he sought Lesage's assistance for the designs of Madame de Montespan.'

The crisis of the year 1675 was more serious. Louis XIV suddenly had great fits of devotion. People with their eyes open saw that he was tiring of his mistress. Madame de Montespan, on the Thursday in Holy Week, had been refused absolution by a priest of her parish. Much put out, she hastened to the curé of Versailles, and spoke to him hotly, but the curé approved of his subordinate's action. And the great voice of Bossuet, which had consistently been upraised against the double adultery, resounded with a new force. 'When we were at Versailles, one fast day, about Easter, Madame de Montespan went away,' writes Mademoiselle de Montpensier. 'Every one was vastly astonished at this retreat. I went to Paris, and saw her in the house where her children were. Madame de Maintenon was with her. She saw nobody. As everybody was on the alert about her return, although nobody seemed to pay any attention to it, it was known that M. Bossuet, then tutor to the dauphin, and at present bishop of Meaux, went there every day muffled in a grey cloak.' We have other information from Bossuet's private secretary, the Abbé Le Dieu. Louis XIV ordered his mistress to retire. When Bossuet went to see the exiled lady, she 'loaded him with reproaches; she told him that his pride had urged him to get her driven away, that he wanted to make himself sole master of the king's mind.' Then, when she understood that her wrath smote in vain against the serene firmness of the prelate, 'she sought to win him by flatteries and promises; she dangled before his eyes the chief dignities in Church and State.'

This exile lasted from April 14 to May 11. On the other hand, the magician Lesage, in an examination held on November 16, 1680, declared that 'if he were in the last torments, he could tell nothing except that in 1675, at the beginning of summer (the exact date), when Madame de Montespan was trying to maintain her position, La Voisin and La Desœillets worked or pretended to work for her; but in reality, powerless to keep for her the love of the king, they merely gave her powders which, taken in certain doses, would have acted as poison.' So Lesage said; and the declarations of the girl Monvoisin, summed up by La Reynie, are identical: 'The powders her mother sent to Madame de Montespan were love powders to be given to the king. Once when her mother took some powders to Clagny she was accompanied by the magician Latour, her eldest brother, a servant named Marie, since dead, and Fernand, a good friend of Latour, and La Vautier; but these did not enter Clagny. She could not say if Latour went in with her mother, but they all came back together, and had lunch at the sign of the *Heaume*, near the Bois de Boulogne, with violins; they made some noise among them. Her brother, who told her about it, told her that her mother brought back fifty louis-d'or. Her mother, besides the powders she gave to Madame de Montespan, did not send any except by Mademoiselle Desœillets, who was the go-between for that purpose. As to the powders which had passed beneath the chalice, they came from a priest called the Prior (the Abbé Guibourg). As to the others which had not been under the chalice, her mother kept them in the drawer of a cabinet of which she had the key. There were black ones, white, and grey, which she mixed in the presence of Desœillets. Her father once wanted to break the cabinet where the powders were kept, saying that some harm would come of it.' And the result of these practices was, once more, of such a nature as to give confidence in the power of sorcery: Madame de Montespan regained her position with the king. It is true that Madame de Richelieu said, 'I am always there as a third party.' In spite of this 'third party,' Madame de Montespan became the mother of the Comte de Toulouse and Mademoiselle de Blois. Madame de Sévigné writes to her daughter on June 28, 1675: 'Your idea about *Quantova* (Madame de Montespan) is very good; if she cannot recover the old ground, she will push her authority and her greatness beyond the clouds; but she must make sure of being loved all the year round without scruple. Meanwhile her house is filled with the whole court, and her consideration is unbounded.' On July 31, Madame de Sévigné writes again: 'The attachment for *Quantova* is always extreme: it's pretty much in order to vex the curé and everybody else.'

In 1675 Madame de Montespan had been dismissed, from religious scruples; in 1676 she was to be sent away for reasons which furnished her with quite another ground for irritation. The king was then suddenly seized with a terrible hunger for a multiplicity of amours, soon over, sudden, and varied. Madame de Sévigné characterises this strange condition in a picturesque phrase: 'There's a scent of new game in the land of *Quanto*.'[11] At short intervals the Princess de Soubise, Madame de Louvigny, Mademoiselle de Rochefort-Théobon, Madame de Ludres, and no doubt others, succeeded one another in the affections and the bed of the king.

Madame de Soubise makes an amusing appearance in the gallery of royal mistresses. She loved Louis out of love for her husband. After collecting for him all the honours and dignities, the offices and the hard cash that he desired, Madame de Soubise struck her tents and retired in good order. She had made the least possible stir and went back to her husband, who was enchanted with the adventure. The Prince of Soubise thought, with the poet, that a share with Jupiter had no dishonour so long as Jupiter could pay a good price.

These intrigues find a double echo, in the writings of Madame de Sévigné and in the records of the Chambre Ardente. On September 2, 1676, Madame de Sévigné writes: 'The vision of Madame de Soubise has passed quicker than a lightning-flash: they have made it up again. *Quanto* the other day at cards had her head resting familiarly on her friend's shoulder, and we fancied that piece of affectation meant "I am better than ever."' But on September 11 the position has changed. 'Everybody believes that the star of Madame de Montespan is paling. There are tears, unfeigned disappointments, affected cheerfulness, sulks; at last, my dear, it is all over. Some tremble, others rejoice, some wish for immutability, the majority for a dramatic change; in a word, we are all eyes and ears for what the most clear-sighted say.' 'Every one thinks that the king loves her no longer,' we read in a letter of September 30, 'and that Madame de Montespan is embarrassed between the consequences which would follow the return of his favours and the danger of no longer enjoying them—the fear that they are being sought elsewhere. Apart from that, she has not very nicely accepted the position of friend: so much beauty as she still has, and so much pride, find it difficult to come down to second place. Jealousies are keen. Have they ever stopped anything?' Again, on October 15, 1676: 'If *Quanto* had packed up her traps at Easter the year she returned to Paris, she would not have been in her present distress; it would have been sensible to adopt that course, but human weakness is great; one wishes to make the most of the remains of one's beauty, and this economy brings ruin rather than riches.' Madame de Ludres had just succeeded Madame de Soubise.

The anxieties of Madame de Montespan were further enhanced by the brilliance, increasing every day, of a new star in the sky of Versailles. At its rising it had shed a pale, discreet, modest light, but a light which twinkled with little mocking scintillations. The widow Scarron, now become Madame de Maintenon, had been chosen as governess of the children of the king and Madame de Montespan. What strides the governess's fortune had taken in a few years! 'But let us speak of the friend' (Madame de Maintenon), writes Madame de Sévigné on May 6, 1676: 'she is still more triumphant than the Montespan. Everything is submitted to her dominion. All the chamber-women of her neighbour are hers: one hands her the rouge-pot on her knees; another brings her her gloves; a third puts her to sleep; she salutes no one, and I fancy that really she laughs in her sleeve at this servitude.'

Madame de Sévigné thus tells us what was passing at court; Marguerite Monvoisin will tell us what was going on among the sorceresses. 'The daughter of La Voisin,' writes La Reynie, 'says that she has seen this sort of mass celebrated over the body by Guibourg in her mother's house. She helped her mother to get things ready: a mattress on seats, two stools at the sides, on which were candlesticks with candles; after which Guibourg came out of the little side-chamber clothed in his chasuble—white, spotted with black fir-cones—and after that La Voisin brought in the woman on whose body the mass was to be said. Madame de Montespan had this sort of mass said three years ago (*i.e.* in 1676) at her mother's house, where she came about ten o'clock and only left at midnight. And when La Voisin told her that it was necessary for her to fix a time when the other two masses might be said, which were necessary if her affair was to be successful, Madame de Montespan said that she could not find time, that La Voisin would have to do what was necessary to assure success, which she promised her and did, and the masses were said on La Voisin herself by Guibourg.' (This again shows the sincerity of the sorceress in the carrying out of these practices.) 'The girl Voisin having notified all the circumstances of the proceeding, the arrangement of the place, that of the person—she knew Madame de Montespan—the preparations of the priest clothed in his sacerdotal vestments, the terms of the incantation, in which the documents show that the names of Louis de Bourbon and Madame de Montespan were mentioned—the girl Voisin adds that a child had its throat cut at the mass said for Madame de Montespan at her mother's.'

'When I was grown up,' said Marguerite Monvoisin, 'my mother was no longer reluctant to trust me, and I was present at this sort of mass, and saw that the lady was stark naked on the mattress, with her head hanging down, supported by a pillow on an overturned chair, the legs too hanging over, a napkin on the belly, a cross on the napkin, and the chalice on the belly.' She adds that this lady was Madame de Montespan. 'At the mass of Madame de Montespan,' said Marguerite in the course of another examination, 'a child was presented which apparently had been prematurely born, and it was put into a basin. Guibourg cut its throat, poured the blood into a chalice, and consecrated it with the wafer, finished his mass, then proceeded to take the child's entrails. My mother next day carried the blood and wafer to Dumesnil to be distilled, in a glass vessel which Madame de Montespan took away.' These facts were confirmed on October 23, 1680, by the confrontation of Marguerite Monvoisin with Guibourg—with this variation, that Guibourg tried to shuffle on to La Voisin the butchery of the child.

'Guibourg said that it was not true that he had opened the child, because it would have stained his alb: he found the child already opened.

'The girl Voisin, on the contrary, declared that he cut open the heart himself, took out some clotted blood, and put it into the vessel into which the other blood and the rest had been put, which Madame de Montespan took away; and that to make the clotted blood go in, a common glass was broken, which, with its foot knocked off, was made to act as a funnel.

'Guibourg said that he did not open the child's stomach, but that having found it open, he did in fact draw out the entrails and open the heart to get out the blood that was in it, and that he put it into a crystal vase with some portions of the consecrated wafer: the whole was carried off by the lady on whose body he had said mass; and that he always believed the lady was Madame de Montespan.'

This picture is fraught with so much horror that we could not bring ourselves to admit its authenticity if the evidence of Marguerite Monvoisin and the Abbé Guibourg were not corroborated by confessions extorted from other accomplices of these crimes, who were arrested at different dates and examined separately—Lesage, Lacoudraye, Delaporte, Vertemart, Françoise Filastre, the Abbé Cotton—confirmed by the declarations of several witnesses who had picked up, before the trial, fragments of talk which escaped the accused. La Reynie emphasises the fact that the declarations of Lesage and the girl Monvoisin were made at an interval of sixteen months, and without their having had any opportunity during those months of communicating with each other.

On October 11, 1680, La Reynie writes to Louvois, who wished to save Madame de Montespan while prosecuting the charges against the other persons, and proposed, with that end, to withdraw from the case the declarations made under torture by Filastre and the Abbé Cotton, which contained the gravest charges against the favourite: 'It is certain, even if we found a legitimate expedient for concealing from the judges for the present the facts which it would be well to keep secret, even for the sake of justice itself, that these very facts would crop up again from the woman Chappelain, from Guibourg, Galet, Pelletier, Delaporte, and perhaps from several more when under trial.'

On the subject of the deposition made by Guibourg, La Reynie writes: 'It is morally impossible that Guibourg has deceived us in his declaration, and that he invented what he tells about the incantations said in course of the masses on the women's bodies. His mind is not active or consistent enough for such continuous thought as would have been necessary to invent what he had said on this subject, because, even supposing he were capable of such application, he has not enough acquaintance with what goes on in the world, and could not have devised so consistent a story in regard to Madame de Montespan.' Elsewhere he writes: 'Guibourg and the girl Monvoisin have corroborated one another about circumstances so particular and so horrible that it is difficult to conceive two persons being able to imagine and fabricate them unknown to each other. It seems that these things must have occurred, or they could not have been described.'

The illustrious magistrate adds the following reflections:—

'1. The time of the relations of La Voisin with Latour, the journeys to Saint-Germain, and the powders which she made him work at, was the year 1676.

'2. The time of the abominations described by Guibourg and the girl Monvoisin fits the same period.

'3. Two years ago Lesage spoke of Latour, the poisons, Desœillets, and the journeys of La Voisin in 1676.

'4. It was established at the trial that two or three years before Lesage was taken, he testified that he feared the business would ruin him. They said at that time that the king had the vapours. He declared that he wished to leave La Voisin on that account, and because of the dealings she had with Desœillets.

'From the beginning of these inquiries, these same facts have been spoken of; La Bosse, the first to be tried, gave the first inkling of them; she spoke of them under torture; but, because the king had not yet allowed this sort of facts to be collected in regard to persons of consideration, and because there was nothing to make us pay the least attention to them, no mention was made in the report of the torture of La Bosse of what she had said about Madame de Montespan.'

In this year 1676, Madame de Montespan not only had recourse to the incantations of the black mass; at her instigation, the sorceresses sent La Boissière and Françoise Filastre to Normandy to a certain Louis Galet, who had 'fine secrets' in regard to poison and love. Galet gave them powders. As soon as his name was uttered by the prisoner before the Chambre Ardente, an order was given for his arrest. He was flung into prison at Caen on February 23, 1680. While still far away from the other prisoners, detained at Vincennes or the Bastille, he was put through interrogations, and the depositions made by him and the others coincided with remarkable accuracy. And La Reynie's conclusion is: 'Guibourg and Galet having confessed after the torture of La Filastre, they gave between them a complete proof of these facts.'

It must be confessed that Madame de Montespan would have been of a singularly incredulous nature if she had not retained a blind confidence in the influence of the devil as invoked by the magicians and sorceresses. Madame de Ludres was discarded, and Louis fell at Madame de Montespan's feet again. On June 11, 1677, Madame de Sévigné wrote to Madame de Grignan: 'Oh, my daughter, what a triumph at Versailles! what redoubled pride! what a re-entry into possession! I was in the room for an hour. She was in bed, decked out, with her hair done: she was resting for the *medianoche* (supper about midnight). She launched shafts of contempt at poor *Io* (Madame de Ludres), and laughed at her having the audacity to complain of her. Imagine all that an ungenerous pride could make her say in triumph, and you will get near the truth. It is said that the little woman (Madame de Ludres) will resume her ordinary duties about Madame. She went off to walk in perfect solitude with La Moreuil in the garden of the Marshal Du Plessis.' On June 18, Madame de Sévigné wrote to Bussy-Rabutin: 'Madame de Montespan wanted to strangle her (Madame de Ludres), and makes her life terrible.' On July 7, to Madame de Grignan: 'Poor *Isis* (Madame de Ludres) has not been to Versailles. She has remained in her solitude. When a certain person (Madame de Montespan) speaks of her, she says, "that rag." The event makes everything permissible.'

'*Quanto* and her friend Louis XIV are together longer and more eagerly than ever they were. The ardour of the first years has returned, and all fears are banished, all restraint removed, which persuades us that never was empire seen more firmly established.' And a little later: 'Madame de Montespan was the other day covered with diamonds; the brilliance of so blazing a divinity was more than one could bear. The attachment seems greater than ever: they are all eyes for one another: never has love been seen to resume its sway like this.'

Yet, courted and victorious as she was, the favourite appeared a prey to torment; she was agitated, in a terrible fever. On January 13, 1678, the

Comte de Rébenac wrote to the Marquis de Feuquières: 'Madame de Montespan's gambling has reached such a pitch that losses of 100,000 crowns (£60,000 to-day) are common. On Christmas Day she lost 700,000 crowns; she staked 150,000 pistoles (£280,000 at the present day) on three cards, and won.' She lost her head in her triumph—her last triumph, dazzling but ephemeral, and about to be followed by days of cruel anguish.

In March 1679, Madame de Maintenon asked the Abbé Gobelin 'to pray and to have prayers said for the king, who is on the brink of a deep precipice.' This 'precipice' was the heart of Marie Angélique de Scoraille, demoiselle de Fontanges. She was eighteen years old, fair, with glossy flaxen hair; her large eyes, with their look of childish wonderment, were a light grey, deep and limpid; her skin was white as milk, her cheeks a lovely rose-pink; and in disposition, said her contemporaries, she was a genuine heroine of romance. She lived at Court in the capacity of maid of honour to Madame, as Madame de Ludres and Mademoiselle de la Vallière had done before her. 'Mademoiselle de Fontanges,' says Madame Palatine, 'is lovely as an angel, from head to foot.' If we may trust Bussy-Rabutin, 'her relatives, seeing her beauty and grace, and having more love for their fortune than for their honour, clubbed together to fit her out for Court, and to provide her with means corresponding to the position she was entering.'

This was a thunderbolt for Louis XIV and Madame de Montespan. We read in the *Précis historique de Saint-Germain-en-Laye*, by Lorot and Sivry: 'Madame de Montespan left Saint-Germain suddenly because of the jealousy she has conceived for Mademoiselle de Fontanges.' But the royal lover did not allow his mistresses to leave him at their own whim. He had imposed on Louise de la Vallière the bitter martyrdom of following as an expiatory victim the triumph of Madame de Montespan; he now compelled Madame de Montespan to witness the triumph of Mademoiselle de Fontanges. The proud marquise resigned herself to it, at least in appearance. On March 30, 1679, she wrote to the Duke de Noailles: 'All is very quiet here; the king only comes into my room after mass and after supper. It is much better to see each other seldom but pleasantly, than often with embarrassment,' Soon even this apparent satisfaction was withdrawn from her. The desertion was public and complete.

According to Madame de Sévigné, 'there was a ball at Villers-Cotterets, at Monsieur's place. There were masques. Mademoiselle de Fontanges appeared there in great brilliance, and adorned by the hands of Madame de Montespan.' Bussy rejoiced at the disgrace. 'Madame de Montespan has fallen, the king regards her no more, and you may be sure the courtiers follow his example.'

On April 6, Madame de Sévigné wrote: 'Madame de Montespan is enraged; she cried a good deal yesterday, and you may guess the martyrdom her pride is suffering.' On June 15, she replies to her daughter: 'It is an infernal position, as you say, that of her who goes four paces ahead' (alluding to Madame de Montespan).

She launched out into epigrams against her fortunate rival, just as she had satirised Louise de la Vallière. 'Madame de Montespan,' writes Bussy-Rabutin, 'seeing that the great Alcandre (Louis XIV) was drifting away from her more and more every day, became so choleric that she began publicly to abuse Mademoiselle de Fontanges. She told every one that the great Alcandre was surely not very fastidious to love a creature who had had her little love affairs in the country; that she had neither wit nor education; and that, properly speaking, she was only a beautiful painting. She said a thousand other things about her equally irritating. Indeed, she always displayed the same proud spirit which nothing had been able to quell.'

Mademoiselle de Fontanges responded by loading her predecessor and all her children with costly presents. She had just been proclaimed a duchess with an annuity of 20,000 crowns. The fury of Madame de Montespan broke out. She had a violent scene with Louis, and when the king reproached her with her pride, her domineering spirit, and other defects, she replied with haughty scorn, concentrating all the violence of her wrath in one of those hard and bitter words which had made her so much feared in the time of her reign; she answered, 'that if she had the imperfections of which he accused her, at any rate she did not smell worse than he.'

'My mother,' said the girl Monvoisin, 'told me that Madame de Montespan wanted at that time to go to extremities, and tried to induce her to do things for which she had much repugnance. My mother gave me to understand that it was against the king, and after hearing what had passed at the house of Trianon (a sorceress, partner of La Voisin), I could not doubt it.' The deserted mistress resolved to put an end to Louis and Mademoiselle de Fontanges. She applied to the sorceress of Villeneuve-sur-Gravois, and had no difficulty in getting together four accomplices in the terrible room in the Rue Beauregard: these four were La Voisin and La Trianon, who undertook to put Louis out of the way, and Romani and Bertrand, 'artists in poisons,' who promised to kill Mademoiselle de Fontanges. Madame de Montespan gave them money.

The king was to be poisoned first. La Voisin and her associates intended at first to put magic powders, prepared according to the formulae of the conjuring books, on the clothes of the king, or in some place where he was to pass, 'which Mademoiselle Desœillets, the companion of Madame de Montespan, said could be done easily.' The king would die of decline. But after reflection, La Voisin decided on means, the execution of which struck her as more certain. In conformity with the ancient custom of the kings of France, Louis XIV used to receive in person on certain days the petitions presented by his subjects. Everybody was introduced to his presence without distinction of rank or condition. It was resolved to prepare a petition and steep it in powders that had gone under the chalice; the king would take it in his hands and get his death-blow. La Trianon undertook the preparation of the paper, and La Voisin to place it in the hands of the king.

The petition was drawn up. The king's intervention was asked in favour of a certain Blessis, an alchemist whom the Marquis de Termes was keeping confined in his château. La Voisin betook herself to her friend Léger, a *valet de chambre* of Montausier, and asked of him a letter of recommendation to one of his friends at Saint-Germain, who would get her passed in among the first to an audience with the king, so that she might herself hand him her petition. Léger replied that it was unnecessary for her to go to Saint-Germain, as he would undertake to forward the petition by a sure route; but the sorceress insisted on presenting it herself.

The boldness of La Voisin terrified the most courageous of her companions. The majority of them feared, not death, but the horrible tortures reserved by the law for regicides. In order to frighten her, La Trianon cast her horoscope. This document was found among the papers seized on the sorceress by the Chambre Ardente. La Trianon foretold that La Voisin would be implicated in a trial for a crime against the state. 'Bah!' she replied, 'there are 100,000 crowns to be gained.' That was the price agreed upon by La Voisin and Madame de Montespan for the poisoning of Louis XIV.

La Voisin set out for Saint-Germain on Sunday, March 5, 1679, accompanied by Romani and Bertrand. She returned on Thursday, March 9, very much put out: she had not been able to approach the king so as to give him the petition. She could have put it on the table placed near the king for that purpose, but the paper was useless unless it were placed in the king's own hands. She said that she would return to Saint-Germain, and when her husband asked her what the urgency was, she replied: 'I must accomplish my design or perish in the attempt!' 'What! perish!' exclaimed Monvoisin, 'that's a good deal for a piece of paper.'

On Friday, March 10, the 'missionaries'—priests of a community founded by St. Vincent de Paul, which has already been mentioned—paid a visit to the sorceress. La Voisin took fright, and gave the petition to her daughter to burn, which Marguerite did at dawn on Saturday morning. It is needless to say that the paper had always been kept in an envelope, for to touch it, said the sorceresses, would be certain death. On Sunday, March 12, La Voisin was arrested; it was on Monday the 13th that she had meant to return to Saint-Germain. News of the arrest got abroad, and on Wednesday, March 15, Madame de Montespan fled from Court.

In a succession of hasty notes—the sentences are not even completed, and we have filled them out for greater clearness—La Reynie builds up a proof of the attempt on the life of Louis XIV, planned by La Voisin as the instrument of Madame de Montespan:—

'By the depositions of the girl Voisin, Romani, and Bertrand, it is proved that the journey of La Voisin to Saint-Germain was to present the petition: Bertrand wrote it out, went to learn from La Voisin what she had done, learnt that she had been there since Sunday without being able to present it, had brought it back, and was going to return. From this it is evident that the ultimate object of the journey of La Voisin to Saint-Germain was to present the petition.

'La Trianon and La Vautier agree as to the journey. La Trianon noted in her horoscope the state affair, the crime of high treason; when questioned she gave bad answers; among the facts confessed to, denies the petition; if it were an unimportant matter, would have no interest in denying it: must have had an object, which can be nothing else than what the girl Voisin says.

'The journey to Saint-Germain is the more suspicious in that La Voisin, questioned as to her various journeys, has never mentioned that one, and would have made no ado about mentioning it if there were nothing in it.

'To which must be added the confession made by Voisin to her guards in prison, about the fear she had that she would be asked to explain her journey. She said, "God has protected the king!"'

La Reynie adds: 'La Trianon agrees that she told the girl Voisin that the journey to Saint-Germain was the cause of her mother's arrest, that this journey would do her harm, that she would be involved in some affair of state. At the same time, La Voisin did not appear to be pleased with Blessis (and consequently had no reason to make any efforts to secure his liberty). What is still more considerable, La Trianon and the girl Monvoisin agree that the state crime mentioned in the horoscope was the journey to Saint-Germain.' 'Finally,' observes La Reynie, 'this petition has been mentioned at the trial, long before the girl Monvoisin was arrested.' On September 27, 1679, Louvois wrote to Louis XIV: 'Your Majesty will find in this packet what Lesage has said about the journey of La Voisin to Saint-Germain; he cites so many people as witnesses to his allegations that it is difficult to believe he invented them.' And La Reynie gives confirmation: 'Before making her declaration, the girl Monvoisin said something about it to two prisoners who are with her. Finally, she tried to do away with herself by strangling before making these same declarations.'

The assassination of the Duchess de Fontanges was intended to crown the vengeance of Madame de Montespan. La Voisin exclaimed, in regard to this, when dining with La Trianon: 'Oh! what a fine thing is a lover's spite!' Romani and Bertrand were engaged to poison the young lady at the same time that La Voisin was killing Louis *XIV*; but the poisons employed against her were to be less rapid, so that 'she might die a lingering death,' said the accomplices, 'and that it might be said that she had died of grief at the death of the king.'

Romani had planned to disguise himself as a cloth merchant. Bertrand was to follow him as a valet. They were to present their wares to the duchess, and even if she did not take any cloth, 'she would not refrain from taking gloves,' said Romani, 'because those he would bring from Grenoble would be very well made, and ladies never failed to take some of them when they were well made, and the gloves would have the same effect as the piece of cloth.' They actually sent to Rome and Grenoble for gloves of the finest quality, and Romani 'prepared' them according to the recipes of the magicians.

We find among La Reynie's papers a series of little notes which clearly prove the plot against the life of Madame de Fontanges.

A last feature in the case is not the least surprising.

We have just seen that Madame de Montespan fled from Court when she learnt of the arrest of the sorceress and her accomplices. Her terror, and, above all, her fury were extreme. At the moment when her fortune was for ever ruined, when she felt that she herself was lost, she wished at least to have the terrible joy of seeing the Duchess de Fontanges perish at her hands. The sorceress who had been the chief instrument of her passions was about to be interrogated, and would undoubtedly disclose to the attentive eyes of the judges the horrible practices in which the king's mistress had been concerned. It was at this very moment that Madame de Montespan, burning to realise her designs, entered into relations with Françoise Filastre, the friend of La Voisin, and after her the most terrible sorceress in Paris. Filastre was one of those who had devoted their children to the devil, and murdered them immediately after birth. She went to Normandy to find Galet, who has already been mentioned, then went to Auvergne to obtain secrets for 'poisoning without any sign appearing.' Returning to Paris, she took steps to win an entrance to the house of

Madame de Fontanges; but her arrest prevented her from carrying her scheme into execution.

Nature gave to Madame de Montespan the terrible satisfaction she had sought to obtain from magic and poison. On June 28, 1681, the Duchess de Fontanges died at the age of twenty-two, in the abbey of Port Royal. She was carried off by pleuro-pneumonia, tubercular in origin, the action of which was hastened by loss of blood following an accouchement. The young woman died convinced that she had been poisoned, and suspecting her rival. Louis XIV, who had the same idea, feared that the autopsy might reveal the crime, and sought to prevent it; but the relatives insisted on it. The physicians concluded that it was a natural death. But the opinion was still held that Madame de Fontanges had succumbed to poison administered by Madame de Montespan, an opinion echoed by Madame de Caylus, Madame de Maintenon, Madame Palatine, and Bussy-Rabutin.

Before the commissioners of the Chambre Ardente the magician Lesage had allowed the following remark to escape him: 'If Filastre were captured, they would learn some strange things.' She was taken: she denied everything before the commissioners; but on October 1, 1680, while under torture, she confirmed in the most precise manner the revelations made by the prisoners at the Bastille and Vincennes; and on that very day Louis XIV in terror ordered the sittings of the Chambre Ardente to be suspended. On October 17, 1680, Louvois wrote to La Reynie: 'I have received the letters you have done me the honour to write to me, and the king heard them read with pain.' Louis, then, ordered the closing of the Chambre Ardente, and when on May 19, 1681, the sittings were resumed at the entreaty of La Reynie, the judges were forbidden 'to take any steps in regard to the declarations contained in the reports of the torture and execution of La Filastre.' From that day Louis had no further doubts as to the guilt of his mistress. One more proof was to be furnished him.

The name of Mademoiselle Descœillets, Madame de Montespan's maid, recurs on every page of the proceedings. She was continually going backwards and forwards between her mistress and the sorceresses. The prisoners almost all knew her: they spoke of her in the most positive manner. The girl Monvoisin pointed out her house, where she had been several times. Mademoiselle Descœillets had a friend named Madame de Villedieu, who frequently visited the sorceresses, but for her own private ends. When La Voisin was arrested, the two friends talked about the incident.

'How can you be easy in mind when you have been so often to the sorceress?' asked Madame de Villedieu.

'The king will not allow me to be arrested.'

The remark was voluntarily reported by Madame de Villedieu to the detective Desgrez. And, in fact, when La Reynie on October 22, 1680, wrote to Louvois: 'What has been said in regard to Mademoiselle Descœillets at the beginning and repeated at the end is so strong that it is impossible to prevent her from being confronted with the people who have spoken about her,' his words fell on deaf ears at Versailles. When Madame de Villedieu was taken to Vincennes, she said: 'It is astonishing that I am being imprisoned when I went only once to La Voisin, while you leave Mademoiselle Descœillets at liberty, who has been there more than fifty times.'

Louvois at last decided to order Mademoiselle Descœillets to appear, not before the judges, but before himself in his private room. On November 18, 1680, he wrote to La Reynie:—

'Mademoiselle Descœillets declares with marvellous assurance that not one of those who have named her know her, and, to assure me of her innocence, she charged me to urge the king to allow her to be taken to the place where those who have deposed against her are confined. She stakes her life that no one will be able to tell who she is. His Majesty has therefore been pleased to decide that I shall take her to Vincennes next Friday, and bring down Lesage, the girl Voisin, Guibourg, and the other persons who, as you inform me, have spoken of her. The person of whom I have just spoken will enter and show herself to them, and I will ask them if they know her, without naming her to them.'

The result did not justify Louvois' hopes. La Reynie showed at that time that, unknown to him and in spite of his vigilance, some one was holding communication with the prisoners in Vincennes, who were receiving information from without. This 'some one' was Madame de Montespan. No doubt the lieutenant of police took greater precautions on this occasion. The prisoners were not able to receive preliminary coaching, with the result that one and all immediately recognised the favourite's maid.

Mademoiselle Descœillets, moreover, was under great illusions as to the impunity that would be assured to her. Louis XIV did not allow her to appear before the judges, nor even to be confronted with the prisoners, but he had her shut up for the rest of her days in close confinement. The wretched woman died on September 8, 1686, in the general hospital of Tours. And poor Madame de Villedieu, whose only crime was that she was for a moment in the confidence of Mademoiselle Descœillets, was visited with the same fate, because of the necessity of keeping the great secret.

When he learned suddenly of all the crimes with which the woman he had most loved was stained—the woman whom, in the eyes of Europe, he had made queen of the French Court, who was the mother of his favourite children—what were the sentiments and the attitude of King Louis? What passed in his soul, immured, for posterity as for his contemporaries, in that 'terrible majesty' of which Saint-Simon speaks?

About the middle of August 1680, Louvois, who in this dreadful business devoted all his intelligence and all his influence to protect Madame de Montespan, arranged a *tête-à-tête* with the king. Madame de Maintenon anxiously observed them from a distance. 'Madame de Montespan at first wept,' she says, 'threw reproaches upon him, and at last spoke with pride.' At the first moment, under the shock of the king's declarations, Madame de Montespan had been utterly crushed, had burst into tears of confusion and humiliation; then, regaining command of herself, the masterful woman had risen to the height of her pride, with all the force of her passion and her hatred for her rivals. If it was true, she declared, that she had been driven to great crimes, it was because her love for the king was great, and great also were the harshness, cruelty, and infidelity of him to whom she had sacrificed everything. And the king might strike at her, but he could not forget that he would, with the same stroke, injure in the eyes of France and Europe the mother of his children—children who had been made legitimate children of France. Madame de Montespan left this interview irrevocably ruined, but at the same time definitively saved.

We must remember the rank to which Louis had raised his mistress. It was of the utmost importance to him to avoid a scandal. Even by exiling the fallen favourite, thus absolutely disgracing her, he would run the risk of unloosing storms. La Reynie, who, thanks to his genius for reading the hearts of men, knew Madame de Montespan's character thoroughly, warned Louvois: 'We cannot but fear extraordinary scandals, the consequence of which cannot be foreseen.' Louvois, Colbert, and Madame de Maintenon herself united their efforts to soften too violent a fall. Colbert had just betrothed his younger daughter to Madame de Montespan's nephew. We know, moreover, how much the famous statesman had at heart the national greatness to which he had so arduously contributed, and which in his view could not be dissevered from the greatness of the king. Madame de Maintenon had tenderly trained the children of Madame de Montespan, and retained a real affection for them all her life long. Let us add that Louis, with all his faults—his selfishness, his coarseness, his lack of feeling, his mediocre intellect—had at least a high sentiment of the royal dignity, and that in this awful crisis he did not for a moment depart from that calm and tranquil majesty at which all who approached him never ceased to wonder. Madame de Montespan was not driven from Court. She left her splendid apartments on the first floor for apartments remoter from the centre of the king's life. Louis continued to receive her in public, and publicly paid her visits which deceived careless observers; but practised eyes perceived the profound change which had taken place beneath these external appearances. Madame de Sévigné wrote to her daughter that Louis treated Madame de Montespan with harshness; Bussy-Rabutin wrote that he treated her with scorn. Thus began the expiatory martyrdom which lasted for twenty-seven years.

On March 15, 1691, Madame de Montespan retired to Paris, going into the community of St. Joseph which she had founded. Louis granted her a right royal pension, 10,000 pistoles—£20,000 of to-day—a month; but when, in 1692, the double marriage of Madame de Montespan's children, Mademoiselle de Blois and the Duke de Maine, was celebrated with the Duke de Chartres and Mademoiselle de Charolais, Louis did not allow their mother to appear at the ceremony or to sign the contract.

In the early days of her retirement Madame de Montespan had the greatest difficulty in accommodating herself to the calm monotony of her retreat at St. Joseph's. 'She aired her leisure and anxieties,' says Saint-Simon, 'at Bourbon, at Fontevrault, at her estate at Antin, and for years was quite unable to regain repose of mind.' What were these anxieties? Saint-Simon could not explain them; but we are acquainted with them to-day.

Madame de Montespan was much distressed at abandoning the glory of the world; but from the day when the renunciation was made, she threw herself with as much passion into penitence as she had displayed in ambition and love. 'From the moment of her retirement to St. Joseph's,' says Saint-Simon, 'till her death, her conversion never belied itself, and her penitence continually augmented.' She might have been seen then, in the Carmelite convent in the Rue du Faubourg St. Jacques, imploring from her old rival, whom she had so harshly persecuted—the gentle and saintly Louise de la Vallière, Sister Louise de la Miséricorde—the words which give ease of mind and forgetfulness of the past. Though she tenderly loved those of her children whom she had borne to Louis XIV, it was towards the Duke d'Antin, the son she had by the Marquis de Montespan, that she diverted her solicitude, from a sense of duty, and, as Saint-Simon tells us, 'she occupied herself with enriching him.' 'The king had no manner of dealings with her,' writes the great chronicler, 'even through their children. Their attentions were discouraged, they thenceforth saw her only rarely and after having asked permission. The Père de la Tour wrung from her a terrible act of penitence, namely, to beg her husband's pardon and place herself again in his hands. She wrote herself in the most submissive terms, offering to return to him if he would deign to receive her, or to repair to whatever place he pleased to command. To any one who knew Madame de Montespan, this was a sacrifice of the most heroic kind. She had all the merit of it without undergoing the experience. Monsieur de Montespan sent word that he would neither receive her nor lay any commands upon her, and that he never wished to hear her name mentioned for the rest of his life.'

She had no further relations with the Court, the ministers, *intendants*, or judges; she asked nothing of any man, either for her or hers, and employed the vast income she owed to the king in doing good all around her, bestowing alms with ceaseless and unparalleled generosity, and endowing religious foundations. 'Beautiful as the day,' says Saint-Simon, 'till the last hour of her life; though she was not ill, she always fancied that she was, and that she was going to die.' This anxiety encouraged a taste for travelling, and in her travels she always took with her seven or eight persons as a suite. Between her outbursts of piety and the blossoming forth of her charity, incessant remorse thus made its appearance, as well as the continual need she felt of deadening her thoughts. Only Louis XIV, Louvois, and La Reynie could have explained the following page borrowed from Saint-Simon:—

'Little by little she proceeded to give all that she had to the poor. She worked for them several hours a day at humble and rough tasks, to wit, making shirts and other such-like things, and she made those about her work at them too. Her table, which she had loved to excess, became particularly frugal; her fasts were multiplied, her piety interrupted her entertaining and the harmless little card-play at which she amused herself, and at all hours of the day she would leave everything to go and pray in her closet. Her mortification of the flesh was constant: her chemises and sheets were of the roughest and coarsest unbleached linen, but they were concealed under ordinary sheets and underwear. She continually wore steel bracelets and garters, and a girdle of steel which often wounded her; and her tongue, formerly so terrible a member, had its penance also. She was further so tortured by horror of death that she paid several women whose sole employment was to watch her. She lay at night with all the bed-curtains thrown back, with many candles in her room, her watchers around her, and whenever she woke up she wished to find them chatting, playing cards, or eating, to make sure that they did not fall a-nodding.'

The hour so much dreaded at last struck. She had a singular presentiment of it a year beforehand. At the first attack of illness she saw that her end was near. It came on May 27, 1707, at Bourbon.

'She profited by a brief respite from pain to confess and receive the sacraments. Previously she had all her servants, even the humblest, brought in, made public confession of her public sins, and besought pardon for the scandal she had so long given, and even for her fits of temper, with a humility so real and deep and penitent that nothing could have been more edifying. She then received the last sacraments with ardent piety. The dread of death which all her life had so continually troubled her suddenly vanished and troubled her no more. She thanked God in the presence of them all for permitting her to die in a place where she was far away from the children of her sin, and during her illness spoke of them only this once. She was engrossed in the thought of eternity, in some hope of a cure with which they tried to flatter her, and in her condition as a sinner whose fear was tempered by a steady confidence in the mercy of God, with no regrets, solely intent on rendering to Him the sacrifice most pleasing to Him, with a gentleness and peacefulness which accompanied all her actions.'

The courtiers were surprised at the indifference Louis displayed on learning of the death of his sometime mistress. To the Duchess of Burgundy, who remarked on it, he replied that, since he had dismissed her, he had counted on never seeing her again, and that she was from that time dead to him. He openly reproved the grief manifested by Madame de Montespan's children; and, to the stupefaction of the Court, he forbade them to wear mourning, a circumstance the more incomprehensible because at that same date the Princess de Conti, daughter of Louis XIV and Louise de la Vallière, was wearing mourning for Madame de la Vallière her aunt.

It would be unjust to judge Madame de Montespan solely by what has been here said. We have spoken only of the crimes to which she was driven by the violence of her passions. We have not recalled the wealth she distributed with as much liberality as discretion, or the brilliance given to the Court by her grace and wit, or the enlightened protection which the greatest writers and artists found in her, the radiant kindliness with which she sweetened the declining years of the great Corneille—in a word, the innumerable deeds of kindness she performed with as much intelligence as affection, the fruits of some of which remain to this day. It would require a Racine, with his penetrating mind, his ability to reconcile opposite extremes in one and the same character, and the harmonious majesty of his language, to speak of Madame de Montespan. Bright and radiantly beautiful, of queenly elegance, charming by the distinction of her manners and the delicate wit of her conversation, light-hearted and joyous, she dominated the whole Court of France—this horrible client of the Abbé Guibourg, of La Filastre and La Voisin.

III. A MAGISTRATE

Lieutenant of police Gabriel Nicolas de la Reynie was the mainspring of the proceedings against the poisoners. He alone carried through the vast operations, bristling with difficulties. And it would be impossible to find any point of his administration in which his genius and his character appear in a more striking or complete manner. It is thanks to him, and to the careful notes he took daily on the cases of the prisoners, that we have been able to discover the facts of which Louis XIV believed he had destroyed every trace when he ordered the burning of the various documents in his private room.

Saint-Simon, who has utterly shattered reputations which seemed firm as rock, pauses with respect before Nicolas de la Reynie, though the functions with which he was endowed were a subject of genuine abhorrence to him. 'La Reynie, councillor of state,' he writes, 'so well known for having been the first to lift the office of lieutenant of police from its natural low estate, and for making it a sort of ministerial office; a man of great importance too, because of the king's direct confidence in him, his constant relations with the Court, and the number of things in which he is concerned, and in which he has infinite powers of serving or harming in innumerable ways people of the greatest importance, obtained at length in 1697, at the age of eighty, permission to resign so arduous an employment, which he had for the first time ennobled by the equity, moderation, and disinterestedness with which he had fulfilled it, without swerving from the greatest scrupulousness, and doing the least possible injury as seldom as possible; he was, moreover, a man of great virtue and capacity, who in an office which he had, so to speak, created, and in which he was bound to draw upon him the hatred of the public, nevertheless won universal esteem.'

We have a portrait of La Reynie by his friend Mignard, and an admirable etching of the painting by Van Schuppen. Engraving has never reproduced human features with more clearness, colour, and lifelikeness. The face bespeaks a clear, powerful, and well-balanced intelligence; the eyes express a firm and thoughtful kindliness. Such was the La Reynie who investigated the great poison cases.

Though Bazin de Bezons of the French Academy had been associated with him in the Chambre Ardente as examining commissioner, it was the lieutenant of police who did all the work. The number of depositions, interrogatories, confrontations, pleadings, and other documents which he collected is enormous; and we see the magistrate with sure hand cutting a way through this tangled forest, guided by his experience, his knowledge of the human soul, and his clear intellect.

The memorials he has left on questions of the greatest difficulty are useful and interesting to study, because of the method of work they reveal. It is exactly the method which our old professors of rhetoric used to teach for the orderly arrangement of a French dissertation or an historical essay. The principal and fundamental fact is noted down about the middle of the left-hand page, with a large bracket embracing sub-divisions; each of these sub-divisions is in turn accompanied by a bracket embracing sub-divisions of these sub-divisions; and so on to the end of the right-hand page, which is filled from top to bottom with minute and close writing: there you have a multitude of slight facts following one another in methodical order, all focussing on the principal fact, found, as we have said, in the middle of the left-hand page. There is no college student but has built up his schemes for French essays on this model. But there is no question, in La Reynie's portfolios, of rhetorical dissertations or Latin compositions; he deals there with irrevocable sentences about to be pronounced 'on the flesh and blood of men,' to use his own phrase. And if we go from these bracketed plans to the memoirs and reports to which they guided the magistrate's thought, we find ourselves in possession of marvels of clear thinking and judging.

During the long poison case, La Reynie showed himself indefatigable in work. He had no other concern than right and the triumph of justice. And in proportion as the number of criminals increased, and the greatest names in the French nobility and Parlement were found to be compromised by his inquiries—in proportion as relatives, friends, all who feared for themselves, and nobility and Parlement fearing for their honour and their privileges, were up in arms against him, his courage grew, his activity redoubled; he pushed on his inquiries, urging the king, urging the ministers, demanding new warrants, fresh arrests, seeking permission to extend his formidable investigations over an ever-widening circle.

Sorceresses and magicians thronged about the royal Court like swarms of wasps about a hive of honey. In this monstrous hive were concentrated the wealth and honours which awoke and stimulated the ambitions and passions in which the sorceresses found their booty.

The sorceresses had little lodgings at Saint-Germain, Fontainebleau, Versailles, around the palaces. They won admission to the Court as fruit-sellers or dealers in perfumes distilled by the magicians; they offered pastes for softening the skin and waters for improving the complexion. They allied themselves with the domestics of great houses, and domiciled themselves with the laundresses connected with them. They were intimates of those persons who hung about the Court with the curious profession of presenters of petitions. They sometimes even entered the service of a duke or a marchioness. La Chéron was with Monsieur de Noailles and Monsieur de Rabaton in succession. La Vigoureux was actively engaged in finding places for serving-maids and lackeys. We have seen the relations between the fortune-tellers and Leroy, governor of the pages of the Petite Ecurie. Girardin, governor of the dauphin's pages, was connected with the magician Belot. Blessis, a crony of La Voisin, was presented to the queen by Madame de Béthune, by the queen to the dauphin, and by the dauphin to the king.

Among the *bourgeoises* of Paris who were struck at by the depositions of the fortune-tellers we have indicated the principal ones, and then, coming to the Court ladies, the most illustrious of all, Madame de Montespan. But how many others La Reynie had to deal with! The beautiful Duchess of Orleans, Henrietta of England, was accused, not without the greatest probability, of having had a mass said against her husband, with the incantations of sorcery, in the Palais-Royal itself. Madame de Polignac and Madame de Gramont tried to get Louise de la Vallière poisoned. The Countess de Soissons, Olympe Mancini, who had inspired Louis XIV with his first passion, was compromised so deeply that, warned by the king, she fled into the Netherlands. Louis XIV said to the Princess de Carignan, Madame de Soissons' mother: 'I was determined that the countess should escape; perhaps some day I shall render an account therefor to God and my people.'

When Madame de Montespan was at the height of her power, rivals, jealous of her good fortune, applied to the sorceresses for formulae and powders to 'send her packing,' just as she had done with the idea of getting rid of La Vallière. These were the Duchess of Angoulême, Madame de Vitry, and her own sister-in-law, Antoinette de Mesmes, Duchess de Vivonne. The practices to which this last had recourse were precisely the same as those with which the secret life of Madame de Montespan has acquainted us. She applied to La Filastre and La Chappelain, who were also employed by the dazzling mistress of the king. The sorceresses did not hesitate between the two sisters-in-law, thinking to come off well either way: if the one wished to retain the affection of the king, the other sought to possess herself of it, and in either case money would fall into their purses. Louis did not allow the Duchess de Vivonne to be proceeded against, related so closely as she was to Madame de Montespan. It is probable also that he was dissuaded from it by Colbert, who had married one of his daughters to the Duke de Mortemart, son of the duchess.

We may imagine the emotion, agitation, and anxieties aroused at Court and in Paris by the prosecutions directed by the Chambre Ardente against so large a number of persons belonging to the most distinguished families: the arrests of Mesdames de Dreux and Leféron, of Poulaillon and the Abbé Mariette, relatives of the chief magistrates; the warrants issued against the Duchess de Bouillon, the Princess de Tingry, the wife of Marshal la Ferté, the Countess de Roure; the hasty flight out of the kingdom of the Marchioness d'Alluye, the Viscountess de Polignac, the Count Clermont-Lodève, the Marquis de Cessac, the Countess de Soissons; the imprisonment in the Bastille of the famous Marshal de Luxembourg, who had employed magicians to beg the devil to remove his wife. 'Every one is agitated,' wrote Madame de Sévigné, on January 26, 1680, 'every one is sending for news and going into houses to pick them up.'

Further, the public imagination was impressed; crimes were the stock topic of conversation. The most trifling accidents were attributed to poison. Every husband was accused of poisoning his mother-in-law. Terror reigned in Paris.

Then there was a reaction. Nobles and lawyers displayed equal irritation at the Chamber's daring to push its investigations the length of them. Were rank and name no longer a rampart high enough against the inquisitions of a lieutenant of police? There was an end to society. The result was, that ere long the only person in the whole matter who appeared really criminal in the eyes of people of importance was La Reynie himself. 'To-day,' says Madame de Sévigné, 'the cry is, the innocence of the accused and the horrid scandal! You know this sort of parrot cry. Nothing else is talked about in any company. There is scarcely another example of such a scandal in any Christian court.' And some days later, playing sedulous echo to the general gossip, the charming marchioness said it was a shame to haul up people of position for such a pack of nonsense. 'The reputation of Monsieur de la Reynie is abominable,' she wrote to her daughter on May 31, 1680; 'what you say is exactly to the point; his being alive proves that there are no poisoners in France.' La Reynie had just discovered, indeed, a plot to murder him.

The reader will remember the demonstration organised against the lieutenant of police at the time of the liberation of Madame de Dreux, who was carried off in triumph between her husband, the *maître des requêtes*, and her lover, Monsieur de Richelieu. The nobility got up a similar demonstration when Marie Anne Mancini, Duchess de Bouillon, appeared before the Chambre Ardente. She had done her best to find means of quickly ridding herself of her husband, so that she might marry the Duke de Vendôme. The Duke de Bouillon was informed of it by Louis himself. Yet the duke accompanied his wife on January 29, 1680, to the Arsenal, giving her his right hand, while the Duke de Vendôme gave her his left: an exact repetition of the scene when Madame de Dreux left the Chambre Ardente between her husband and Monsieur de Richelieu.

Madame de Sévigné has noted down the details of this merry frolic. Madame de Bouillon arrived in a coach drawn by six horses, seated between her husband and her lover, followed by twenty other coaches, packed full of the smartest noblemen and daintiest ladies of the Court. The Marquis de la Fare confirms this account: 'The Duchess de Bouillon made a proud and confident appearance before the judges, accompanied by all her friends, who were in large numbers, and a most distinguished crowd.' 'Madame de

Bouillon entered the Chambre like a little queen,' says Madame de Sévigné; 'she sat down on a chair prepared for her, and instead of replying to the first question, she asked that what she wanted to say might be written down: which was, that she only came there out of respect for the king; she had none at all for the Chambre, which she did not recognise; and that she did not mean to allow any derogation to the ducal privilege.' (This privilege consisted in the right of not being tried except by all the courts united in Parlement.) 'She would not say a word till that was written down, and then she took off her glove and showed a very beautiful hand. She replied honestly enough until her age was asked.

'"Do you know La Vigoureux?"

'"No."

'"Do you know La Voisin?"

'"Yes."

'"Why do you wish to do away with your husband?"

'"I do away with him? Why, you have only to ask him if he thinks so; he gave me his hand to this very door."

'"But why did you go so often to La Voisin's house?"

'"I wanted to see the Sibyls she promised to show me; that company would be well worth all my journeys."

'She was asked if she had not shown the woman a bag of money. She said "No," and for more than one reason, and this she said with a very mocking and disdainful air.

'"Well, gentlemen, is that all you have to say to me?"

'"Yes, madam."

'She rose and said aloud as she went out, "Really, I should never have believed that clever men could ask so many silly questions."

'She was received by all her friends and relatives with adoration, she was so pretty, naïve, natural, bold, so pleasant in appearance and so quiet in mind.' One of the replies she made to La Reynie, who asked her if she had really seen the devil at the sorceress's, was: 'I see him now: he is ugly, old, and disguised as a councillor of state.' This soon got abroad outside the Chambre, and set all Paris and the Court in good humour.

The charges against the Duchess de Bouillon were, nevertheless, very serious. It was proved to the commissioners that she had asked the sorceresses to poison the Duke de Bouillon or to procure his death by witchcraft. Madame de Sévigné thought the matter of little importance. 'The Duchess de Bouillon,' she wrote to her daughter, 'went and asked La Voisin for a little poison to get rid of an old husband who was boring her to death, and an invention to marry a young man who wanted her, without any one knowing it. This young fellow was Monsieur de Vendôme, who took her to the Arsenal holding one hand, Monsieur de Bouillon holding the other. When a Mancini only commits a folly like that, it is winked at; these sorceresses do the thing seriously, and horrify all Europe about a trifle.' Louis XIV took a more severe view of it, and decided that Madame de Bouillon should be confronted with La Voisin. The pretty face of the young duchess became graver when she heard this, and she begged to be spared this indignity. The king complied, but exiled her to Nérac, whence he would not allow her to return, in spite of the entreaties of her many friends.

The revelations which ensued before the Chambre struck a more cruel blow at La Reynie's soul than the anger of the world. Wrapped in his consciousness of rectitude, he heard cries and threats only as the faint murmurs of a distant mob.

Three sentiments dominated him and guided his whole life: the religious sentiment, which declared itself in a strong, sane, simple piety, the piety of a man possessing a quiet conviction of the truth of his faith; love for his king, a love composed of respect and admiration, with shades of affection like that of a son for a father, and allied also to a religious veneration; finally, a high sentiment of his judicial office with an immovable respect for justice. His worship of the king extended to all that concerned and surrounded him, to all that he loved and honoured. The greatness of Louis XIV is easily explained, in spite of his personal mediocrity, when we see with what passion and by what men he was served. The revelations about Madame de Montespan, the mother of the king's children, the woman who had almost won a seat on the throne of France, were anguish to La Reynie. It is touching to see his grief becoming more keen, more poignant, as evidence accumulated and conviction forced itself upon his mind. 'Private facts,' he writes at the head of a memorandum in which the charges against Madame de Montespan are summed up, 'which were painful to listen to, the idea of which is so grievous to recall and which are still more difficult to relate.' In the light of these revelations his judgment, usually so clear, precise, and sure, became confused, and being unable to believe what he saw, he fancied that his own vision was becoming imperfect. 'I recognise my weakness. In spite of myself, the nature of these private circumstances (those concerning Madame de Montespan) impresses my mind with more fear than is reasonable. These crimes scare me.' Then he recurs to the documents with judicial composure. 'These are the very deeds we must look upon and draw our inferences from.' But it was just the inferences deduced from these actions that his mind could not admit. 'I recognise that I cannot pierce the thick darkness with which I am surrounded. I ask for time to think more about it; and perhaps it will happen that, after much thinking, I shall see even less than I see now. After well considering everything, I have found no other course to suggest than to seek for further enlightenment, and to await the aid of Providence, which has drawn from the feeblest imaginable beginnings the knowledge of this infinite number of strange things it was so necessary to know. All that has happened hitherto leads us to hope (and I do hope with great confidence) that God will at length reveal this abyss of crime, that He will at the same time show the means to escape from it, and inspire the king with all that he ought to do in a matter of such importance.'

In studying these reports of La Reynie to Louvois, we discover a circumstance as impressive as curious. In the course of his memoranda, the magistrate clearly and logically unfolds the reality of the charges against the favourite, but when in closing it falls upon him to draw practical conclusions, his mind shrinks from the task, his thought takes fright like a horse shying before an unexpected obstacle. 'I have done what I could, when I examined the proofs and the presumptions, to assure myself and remain convinced that the facts are genuine, and I could not succeed. I have sought, on the other hand, everything that might persuade me that they were false, and that too has been impossible.'

His distress was augmented by the conflict which arose in his conscience between the duties he owed to justice and those he owed his king. 'At that time when my mind was so cast down,' he wrote, 'I besought God in His mercy to permit me to preserve the fidelity I owed to my office, and to enable me to walk sincerely in all that it pleased the king to command me.' Louis XIV ordered that a portion of the case should be withdrawn from the cognisance of the judges. The blow was so hard to La Reynie that his strength of mind wellnigh failed under it. 'I hope,' he wrote to Louvois on October 17, 1681, 'that his Majesty in his favour and goodness will have compassion on my weakness when he considers that, with the fear and respect I could not fail to be in, occupied moreover and filled with the idea of a judge who, in giving a decision contrary to the truth, should judge and be a party to a judgment involving the life of men, I could not at the moment recognise the false position in which I was, nor represent to his Majesty that the affair in question was in the nature of the case not susceptible of the proposed expedient.'

For a moment his resolution seems to have been taken: he would put himself blindly and unreservedly in the hands of the king who had received from God, he writes, higher lights than those of other men; but the next instant the judge reappears in him and determines him, alone, unaided, subordinate official as he was, to enter into a struggle against the powerful ministers supported by the will and favour of the king.

At this moment his character reveals itself in all its greatness.

He went straight to Louis XIV and laid before him the charges against his mistress; then he wrote energetically to Louvois: 'In spite of all the care that has been taken, all these facts (against Madame de Montespan) have cropped up so often, in so many different quarters, and with so many details, that the king has been obliged to allow the interrogation of the prisoners about the favourite, but in private.'

Louvois, one of the most intimate and well-liked friends of Madame de Montespan, did everything he could to save her. Madame de Maintenon, indeed, was hostile to her, and he feared her growing favour. Besides, as the Venetian ambassador observes, Louvois 'worshipped the French monarchy, to which everything seemed to him subordinate.' He felt bound to protect the prestige of the crown against the injury which the condemnation of the favourite would do it. Finally, in defending her, he thought he would ingratiate himself with Louis.

Louvois endeavoured to bring La Reynie over to his views, to persuade him, at first gently, that it was important that the examining judge should find Madame de Montespan innocent. Louvois spoke, urged, demonstrated: La Reynie listened, but did not heed. The minister then changed his tone. He sought to prove to the magistrate that Madame de Montespan must really be innocent. He went to Paris on February 15, 1681, to explain the matter to him. Had not Mademoiselle Descœillets, the favourite's maid, written that 'she was not guilty, and that what he (La Reynie) had been told about her dealings with La Voisin could not be true; that there were twenty women about Madame de Montespan, of whom eighteen hated her, and that they might be asked for information about her, but she thought that the Countess de Soissons had two maids, one of whom was almost her own height, and that the countess might well have taken her name (the name of Mademoiselle Descœillets), to injure both her and Madame de Montespan, whom she hated.'

La Reynie replied that all that was wanted was to confront the young lady with the prisoners at Vincennes. We have already shown that the confrontation took place and that Mademoiselle Descœillets was recognised. Louvois had perforce to devise another defence, to which the inflexible La Reynie made answer: 'After reflecting on what Mademoiselle Descœillets said to Monsieur de Louvois at Vincennes, about her having a niece who was very often with the sorceresses, and who might easily have been mistaken for her, I think it doubtful, because she only said so after having been recognised by the prisoners, and because Madame de Villedieu her good friend, who is at Vincennes, and had had warnings, tried to mislead us in the same way; it appears a concerted plan; and when I asked her what Mademoiselle Desœillets was like, she told me that she was small, short, and well-developed, which is a false description and exactly fits the niece.'

When it was pointed out to La Reynie that La Voisin had denied all knowledge of Mademoiselle Desœillets, he replied: 'The denial of La Voisin, persisted in till her death, must be the more suspicious in that it was so obstinately kept up, because it is now proved that they had dealings together. If Mademoiselle Desœillets herself denies these dealings, that itself can only increase the suspicion.'

Louvois dwelt also on a retractation made by La Filastre after her conversation with her confessor at the moment of going to execution; but the lieutenant of police replied: 'The declaration made by La Filastre exonerating Madame de Montespan applies solely to the poisoning of Mademoiselle de Fontanges. There are two other facts: that of the mass said over her by Guibourg, and further, the agreement between them in regard to the powders prepared by Galet for the king, in which Madame de Montespan was named; and the charges founded on these two facts do not depend wholly on what was said under torture, but were confirmed afresh by the same declaration in which La Filastre retracted the first charge.'

La Reynie thus defended himself and justice, and soon, strong in the rights of the law, he went on from defence to attack. He revealed to the minister the relations which several of the Vincennes prisoners who were mixed up in Madame de Montespan's affair had had with persons of the Court.

These had given instruction and counsel. La Reynie condemned these manœuvres before the very minister who, at the instigation of the king, had been their author.

'And several of these prisoners of rank,' he added courageously, 'have found means of having some of the charges brought against them withdrawn.'

La Reynie was not satisfied with denying the innocence of Mademoiselle Desœillets; he told Louvois: 'It is difficult for her to be left at liberty after such charges. Apprised of all that has been said against her, she is busy taking measures to render her conviction impossible, and she will take these measures along with other ill-disposed persons.'

In case he should not be authorised to arrest her, La Reynie asks that he may at least be permitted to proceed to her examination; and he sketches for Louvois a very skilful plan, showing the ingenious and subtle means by which, without violence or scandal, the confidante might be induced to reveal the truth.

It is hardly necessary to say that these propositions were rejected by Louis and his minister. The magistrate, nevertheless, persevered in the path he had marked out for himself, even after Louvois, to overcome his scruples, had enlisted the assistance of Colbert, the second of the all-powerful ministers.

Boileau once said: 'I admire Monsieur Colbert's inability to endure Suetonius because Suetonius had revealed the infamy of the emperors.' There we have the explanation of his conduct, apart from the personal interest he had in the innocence of Madame de Montespan.

Colbert had only followed at a distance the work of the commissioners of the Chambre Ardente, and he knew only vaguely the charges brought against the king's mistress. He applied to a celebrated advocate of the time, Maître Duplessis, for a statement establishing the innocence of Madame de Montespan, and indicating means of quashing the unhappy proceedings. Colbert even did his best to supply him with arguments.

Duplessis drew up the statement desired. Colbert acknowledged its receipt on February 25, 1681: 'I have seen and examined with care the memorandum you have sent me; I have to receive another to-morrow on the second charge (the attempted poisoning of Mademoiselle de Fontanges), which is no less serious than the first (the attempt on Louis XIV by means of the petition), and the disproof of which is, in my opinion, more complete and perfect.' And Duplessis sent him a second statement with these words: 'Have the goodness to look at the general observation at the beginning, because it may provide answers to many things which appear sufficiently well proved.' The memorials of Duplessis, backed up by Colbert, had no more effect on La Reynie than the arguments of Louvois. The advocate and the minister asked that the prisoners should be dealt with summarily by the Chambre, that torture should not be applied so that they might not reveal the gravest facts, and that as soon as the case had been rapidly despatched, all the documents should be burnt forthwith. But La Reynie said that it was impossible not to follow the rules of justice, and that the Chambre could only judge according to custom and law.

The Chambre Ardente was in a quandary. On the one hand it saw the necessity of yielding to the absolute refusal of Louis to authorise the reading in court of the documents in which Madame de Montespan was concerned; on the other, there was the no less absolute refusal of La Reynie to allow the judges to pronounce a sentence in which all the guarantees custom gave the accused were not respected. It seemed a complete deadlock. The king had gradually allowed himself to be led very far from the resolutions of rigorous equity which he had at first displayed. He had violated the secrets of the documents so far as to communicate to persons of note such parts of the reports of the investigations as concerned them; he had connived at the flight of the Prince de Clermont-Lodève, the Countess de Soissons, and many others. He had trembled at the thought of what revelations La Voisin might make: 'I explained to the king,' wrote Louvois to Bazin de Bezons on December 3, 1679, 'of the reasons you and the commissioners have for beginning the investigation of La Voisin's case, but his Majesty did not give his approval; and this evening I shall give orders to Boucherat and La Reynie not to bring it into court.'

On July 18, 1680, Louvois wrote to La Reynie from Montreuil-sur-Mer: 'The king has not thought fit to give the order you request that the commissioners may be authorised to give judgment in case of necessity, his Majesty not regarding it as seemly that the Chambre should judge prisoners in his absence.' In spite of the efforts made to enwrap the sittings at the Arsenal in impenetrable secrecy, public opinion was not deceived, and we find evidence in many private letters that the king was preventing the prosecution of 'people of the Court.' 'You are aiming at riff-raff,' exclaimed Lalande, one of the prisoners, in open court on July 31, 1681, 'and you ought to aim higher.'

At length, as we have seen, after the declaration of La Filastre on October 1, 1680, the sittings of the Chambre were suddenly suspended.

'This day, October 1, 1680, in execution of the decree of September 30 of the said year, which condemned Françoise Filastre and Jacques Joseph Cotton to death, they have been put to torture ordinary and extraordinary; but the said Filastre having made, both at and apart from torture, declarations of great importance, and the king having seen the report containing fresh declarations made by her in the chapel of the said château of the Bastille before going to execution, his Majesty, for considerations important to his service, was unwilling that the said matters should be laid in gross before the Chambre, and gave orders to Monsieur Boucherat, President of the said court, to close the sittings.'

From that day there was open conflict between the lieutenant of police on the one hand and the ministers supported by all the ladies and courtiers on the other. 'The king,' wrote La Reynie's secretaries, 'was strongly urged by the courtiers, and even by persons in high places, to close the Chambre entirely, under various pretexts, the most specious of which was that a longer investigation of the poisoning cases would bring the nation into discredit abroad.' La Reynie pleaded in answer the respect due to justice, the duty incumbent on the king to have the greatest criminals who had ever appeared in his kingdom brought to trial and punished, and finally, the necessity of purging France of these appalling practices in poison and sacrilege, which had taken in a few years proportions that no one would have conceived possible. He went to Versailles and talked to the king for four days in succession, and for four hours each day. It is a pity that we have no record of the words he addressed to the king and his ministers. Single-handed, he vanquished them all.

'Monsieur de la Reynie having been heard by the king in his cabinet, in presence of the Chancellor and Monsieur de Colbert and the Marquis de Louvois, on four different days, and for four hours each day, his Majesty at length resolved on the continuation of the Chambre, and ordered Monsieur de la Reynie to continue his ordinary investigations; nevertheless, to take no steps on any of the declarations contained in the reports of the torture and execution of La Filastre, which his Majesty, for considerations relating to his service, does not wish to be divulged.'

The court sitting at the Arsenal resumed its labours on May 19, 1681, but on the condition laid down by the king that nothing further should be done in regard to the declarations in which Madame de Montespan had been involved. On December 17, the facts which he had wished to keep from the knowledge of the judges reappeared with new force at the examination of La Joly. Louvois at once wrote to Bazin de Bezons, the fellow-commissioner of La Reynie, instructing him to be careful to put all these declarations into separate portfolios not to be shown to the judges. La Reynie in fact perceived that the difficulties of the Court, in regard to a regular performance of its duties, were increasing from day to day, and it was not long before he understood, and made his colleagues see also, that the mere fact of the suppression of the report containing the replies of Filastre under torture rendered it impossible to investigate legally the cases of the principal prisoners. This he clearly demonstrated in notes really admirable in their outspokenness and sound judgment. And to measure their dignity and courage, we must remember that his words were addressed directly to Louvois and Louis XIV. But Louis' character was not great enough to allow him to sacrifice his pride to the public good, to consent to such a humiliation in the eyes of his subjects and of Europe. He adhered to his veto on the communication of the Montespan documents to the Chambre. On his part, La Reynie remained inflexible, refusing to allow a case to be tried in which the whole of the documents were not submitted to the court. Yet something had to be done: a Chamber must be either open or shut.

After having done everything possible to enable justice to follow its course in complete independence, so as to reach the guilty however high-placed they were, La Reynie indicated the only solution which would permit the magistrates—since they were not allowed to fulfil their duty to the full—not to fail in so much of their duty as lay in the limited field still open to them.

There were at that time in France tribunals in which judges sat, and *lettres de cachet* which operated without legal formalities, at the mere command of the king. Elsewhere we have shown how, almost at the same period, d'Aguesseau, the most illustrious of French judges, asked for *lettres de cachet* in the course of a case in which he was engaged. Like d'Aguesseau, La Reynie might have said: 'I am not accused of a fondness for extraordinary ways and a hatred of the forms known to justice, yet I find here many reasons for having recourse to orders from the king' (*lettres de cachet*).

'His Majesty being unwilling to give the Chambre cognisance of certain facts,' he wrote on April 17, 1681, to Louvois, 'or that it should try certain prisoners and certain accused parties, reserving them to himself because of their importance, to deal with them through his own justice and the other means he proposes to make use of, it seems to me that we can arrive at the end the king is aiming at by very simple methods, and there can be no objection since the commissioners of the Chambre will have no knowledge of the matters concerning which they are not to be judges.'

What was required, according to La Reynie, was to give up the investigation of the cases of those who had knowledge of facts implicating Madame de Montespan; and since it was impossible to try them according to the rules of justice, to be satisfied with imprisoning them under *lettres de cachet* in the royal fortresses. In face of the attitude taken up by La Reynie in refusing to proceed to a judgment which would violate the traditional forms and the securities they granted to the accused, the king and his ministers had perforce to yield.

La Reynie enumerates a long list of the criminals charged with monstrous crimes who hoped by this means to escape the rigour of trial, the anguish of torture and death by the stake or the gibbet, and he adds:—

'There are 147 prisoners at the Bastille and Vincennes; of this number there is not one against whom there are not serious charges of poisoning or dealings in poison, and further charges of sacrilege and impiety. The majority of these criminals are likely to escape punishment.

'La Trianon, an abominable woman, in regard to the nature of her crimes and her dealings with poison, cannot be tried, and the public, in losing the satisfaction of an example, is no doubt losing also the fruit of some new discovery and the total conviction of her accomplices.

'Nor can the woman Chappelain be tried, because La Filastre was confronted with her: a woman of large connection, long devoted to the study of poisons, suspected of several poisonings, continually practising impieties, sacrilege, and sorcery; accused by La Filastre of having taught her the practice of her abominations with priests; deeply implicated in the case of Vanens.

'For the same reasons, Galet cannot be tried; although a peasant, a dangerous man, and dealing openly in poisons.

'Lepreux, a priest of Notre Dame, engaged in the same practices as La Chappelain, accused of sacrificing the child of La Filastre to the devil.

'Guibourg—this man, who cannot be compared to any other in regard to the number of his poisonings, his dealings with poison and sorcery, his sacrilege and impiety, knowing and known by every notorious criminal, convicted of a great number of horrible crimes—this man, who has mutilated and sacrificed several children; who, apart from the sacrilege of which he is convicted, confesses to inconceivable abominations; who says he has practised by diabolical means against the life of the king; of whom we hear every day new and execrable things, and who is loaded with accusations of crimes against God and king—he, too, will assure impunity to other criminals.

'His concubine, the woman Chanfrain, guilty with him of the murder of some of her children, who has shared in some of Guibourg's sacrifices, and who, according to appearances and the turn the case was taking, was the infamous altar on which he performed his ordinary abominations, will also remain unpunished.

'There is also a large number of other accused persons who will remain free from punishment for their crimes. The girl Monvoisin cannot be tried, nor Mariette, whatever may come to light about him. Latour, Vautier, and his wife will not only remain unpunished, but, for considerations prompting to the concealment of their secret crimes, their case will not be heard through.'

La Reynie says further, not without a touch of melancholy: 'In all this there is reason to wonder at the providence of God. If Mariette had been captured before the trial of La Voisin, and they had spoken about the business of Madame de Montespan, this monster (La Voisin) would have escaped justice, and La Filastre also, if she had put forward what she said at her torture.'

It remained to close the Chambre without too great a shock to public opinion, or leading people to believe that after so much noise the whole thing was to be smothered. 'We must wind up the Chambre,' writes La

Reynie, 'but we must avoid doing so with an appearance of weariness and disgust combined, so that the large number of persons interested may not find occasion to discredit justice, and so that the wicked people who remain, known or unknown, may not cease to be in terror, or, losing their fear, recommence their ill-deeds with the same freedom as they had before.'

The magistrates who composed the Chambre were themselves keenly desirous that its closing should be announced. Among other reasons, the lieutenant of police gives their reluctance and aversion to condemn, 'a reluctance which good men cannot help feeling,' and their sorrow at not being able to try the principal offenders.

It was important, then, not to appear to close the Chambre from any feeling of weariness, and above all not to awake any suspicion of the real causes at work. The public was already murmuring. Compelled as they were, on account of the complicity of Madame de Montespan, to allow all the accused who had had dealings with La Voisin to go scot-free—to wit, the Abbé Guibourg, Lesage, and other guilty persons—the judges took up again the case of Vanens, which had lain dormant. But here again the principal actor, Vanens, escaped the rigour of the law through his connection with the favourite. The commissioners of the Chambre had the good luck to find unexpectedly, in one of the reports, a denunciation against a certain Pinon du Martroy, a councillor to the Parlement, who had been involved in the disgrace of Fouquet. At the time when judgment had been passed on the financiers after the fall of Fouquet, the goods of Pinon had been seized, and Guibourg said that, to wreak vengeance and secure Fouquet's release from prison, he had performed incantations against the king, as well as practised sorcery. Pinon was dead, but he was said to have had a confidant in Jean Maillard, auditor to the exchequer. This man was secured, and as he occupied a prominent position, his case created a great sensation. He was condemned on February 20, 1682, for having 'known and not revealed the detestable designs formed against the person of the king.' The councillor denied everything at his torture, and adhered to his denial till the moment of his death. It is certain that among the various accusations brought before the commissioners of the Chambre Ardente, those directed against Maillard are among those that were least fully proved. The execution took place on February 21, and, contrary to custom, at midday.

It was followed on July 16, 1682, by that of La Chaboissière, Vanens' valet. This wretch was condemned to be hanged after preliminary torture. He was less guilty than Vanens, of whom he had only been the tool; but his low rank had put him beyond the pale. Then the proceedings were brought to a close in due form, without any appearance of a serious miscarriage of justice in the eyes of the crowd. The Chambre Ardente was finally closed by a *lettre de cachet* of July 21, 1682.

La Reynie did not consider that his work was yet done. In his correspondence with Louvois, he had constantly harped on the idea that they should profit by the experience gained during the long investigations of the court to avoid the recurrence of such crimes. He was intrusted, along with Colbert, with the drafting of an order. On August 30, 1682, appeared the famous edict against soothsayers and poisoners, which was the joint work of these two great men; magicians and sorceresses were driven from France, the manufacture and sale of poisons necessary in trade and medicine were regulated by ordinances which have triumphed over time and revolutions, and after two centuries are still in force to-day.

The numerous prisoners whose connection, close or remote, with the machinations of Madame de Montespan safe-guarded them from trial, were transferred under *lettre de cachet* into different fortresses—those which appeared the safest in the kingdom. With excessive precaution, Louvois ordered that each of them should be fastened to his prison by an iron chain, one link of which was to be imbedded in the wall and another fixed to the person of the prisoner.

All these unhappy creatures remained in this condition till their death, some of them for more than forty years. The minister sent the most rigorous instructions to prevent them from holding communication with anybody outside, and to secure that the staff employed in providing for their material and spiritual wants should be reduced to the lowest possible number and composed of persons in whom entire confidence might be placed. And to destroy in advance any effect which the revelations of the prisoners might make on the minds of the governors of citadels and fortresses, Louvois sent these officers word that their new guests were villains who had invented infamous calumnies against Madame de Montespan, the falsity of which had been proved before the Chambre, and that if any of them happened to open his lips on the subject, he was to be answered at once with a sound flogging.

The most important of the prisoners—Guibourg, Lesage, Galet, and Romani—were conveyed to the citadel of Besançon. Guibourg died there three years after his entrance.

Fourteen women were taken to the castle of St. André de Salins. Louvois wrote in regard to them on August 26, 1682, to the lord-lieutenant of Franche-Comté:—

'The king having thought fit to send to the château of St. André de Salins some of the people who were arrested in virtue of warrants of the court that dealt with the matter of the poisons, his Majesty has commanded me to inform you that his intention is that you prepare two rooms in the said château, so that six of these prisoners may be kept safely in each of them, the which prisoners are to have each a mattress in the place arranged for them, and to be fastened either by a hand or a foot to a chain which shall be fastened to the wall, the said chain however to be long enough not to prevent them from lying down. As these people are criminals who deserve extreme penalties, the intention of the king is that they be thus fastened for fear they should injure the people set to guard them, who will go in and out to bring them food and attend to them generally. His Majesty's intention is that you prepare two similar rooms in the citadel of Besançon, so that twelve of the prisoners may be kept securely there. You will observe that these rooms are to be so situated that no one can hear what these people say.'

Auzillon, one of the staff of the provost of the Isle de France, escorted the principal sorceresses, Pelletier, Poulain, Delaporte, the girl Monvoisin, and Catherine Leroy, to the citadel of Belle-Isle-en-Mer.

La Chappelain, the companion of La Filastre, was imprisoned in the castle of Villefranche, where she died forty years later, on June 4, 1724. She lived there in company with another sorceress who, like her, had been withdrawn from the jurisdiction of the Chambre Ardente, and for the same reasons—namely, La Guesdon.

The governor of Villefranche wrote in August 1717, that 'of two old prisoners of state for poison, the survivors of four who had been locked up there for thirty-six years, La Guesdon died on the 15th instant, leaving forty-five livres in silver, which she had saved during that time out of her eight sous a day for food: of these she instructed her surviving companion to take what she needed for her personal use, and to use the balance in paying for prayers for her—this is one pensioner the less for the king. The woman was seventy-six years old; the survivor (La Chappelain) is no younger. They were in the same room.'

Finally, a few prisoners at the Bastille and Vincennes, wholly ignorant of the poison affair, and others whose innocence was recognised by the commissioners of the Chambre Ardente, had been shut up, unluckily for themselves, in the same room with prisoners implicated in the crimes of Madame de Montespan. This chance meeting condemned them to perpetual confinement.

'Manon Bosse,' writes La Reynie, 'was sent to the nuns of Baffens, at Besançon, under the name of Mademoiselle Manon Dubosc, where the king pensioned her to the tune of 250 livres; she was never liberated, because she had been locked up with the daughter of La Voisin, who had told her everything.'

La Gaignière, under the same circumstances, was put in the common workhouse. Nanon Aubert also had been placed with La Voisin's daughter: 'This was the reason that she was not set at liberty, but in 1683 she was placed with the Ursulines of Besançon, and afterwards with those of Vesoul, with orders to say that she was detained for dealings with a lady of quality accused of poison, and she was made to pass for a young lady of rank. The king payed a pension of 250 livres per annum.'

The most characteristic example is that of Lemaire, brother of the woman Vertemart. His complete innocence was absolutely proved. There was no possible charge against him but his having been shut up with the Abbé Guibourg, who 'had told him everything.' On August 4, 1681, Louvois wrote to La Reynie: 'At present Lemaire is not to be set at liberty. I have written to Desgrez what will enable him, if he shows him my letter, to endure his long detention with less pain.' Louvois and Louis XIV were struck by the revolting iniquity of this detention. In August 1682, Louvois sent to Lemaire the considerable sum of 150 pistoles, promising to forward an equal sum every year on condition that he took himself out of the kingdom, never set foot in it again all his life, and spoke to nobody in the world of what he had heard while at Vincennes. If he ever broke one of these engagements, the king would have him seized and incarcerated for the rest of his days.

La Reynie died on June 14, 1709, at the age of eighty years. In his will there is a touching clause which depicts this excellent man to the life. He asks that his body may be interred in the parish cemetery, and not in the church, 'being unwilling that my corpse should be laid in a spot where the faithful assemble, and that the decay of my body should increase the pollution of the air, and thereby endanger the life of ministers and people.' The lieutenant of police, who had devoted a part of his life to the sanitation and good government of the great city confided to his administration, gave an excellent practical lesson on his death-bed, doubtless to the wounding of his dearest sentiments as a Catholic and a believer.

Gabriel Nicolas de la Reynie was in fact a character of rare worth. In our account of him, we have not had to show him as the man of fine culture, the scholar in constant correspondence with Baluze, purchasing and collecting Greek and Latin manuscripts, the skilled patron of the printing-press, the bibliophile to whom we owe the preservation of the original text of Molière. He was a worthy representative of his period, the great epoch in French history. The seventeenth century attained the furthest extremes in good as in evil. It was then that France produced her greatest captains, her greatest statesmen, her most illustrious judges; it was then that the greatest names in literature, art, philosophy, and scholarship dazzled the world; then that the 'daughters of charity' displayed their devotion; that Madame de Chantal diffused around her the sweet perfume of her virtues; but it was then, too, that a Marquise de Brinvilliers extended the boundaries of crime, and an Abbé de Guibourg murdered children upon an altar, over the bare body of a Marquise de Montespan.

THE DEATH OF 'MADAME'[12]

Who has not read Bossuet's funeral oration on Henrietta Anne of England, Duchess of Orleans? Who has not thrilled at the echo of that powerful and poignant apostrophe?—'O woful night! O awful night, when there rang through the air like a sudden thunderclap the amazing tidings, Madame is dying, Madame is dead!... Madame passed from morn to eve like the grass of the field. In the morning she flourished, with what graces you know; in the evening we saw her cut down.... What awful speed! In nine hours the work is accomplished.' Bossuet's masterpiece has crowned the memory of Madame with an immortal halo in which the charms, the quick and exquisite imagination of the young princess, who enchanted her contemporaries,—the lady who set the tone for taste and wit in the midst of the wittiest and most brilliant Court the world has ever known—will shine resplendent through the ages.

The circumstances in which this startling death occurred have aroused the attention of historians. Madame had returned from England, where she had succeeded in getting the Treaty of Dover signed on June 1, 1670, by the ministers of her brother Charles II—the treaty assuring Louis XIV of the alliance of England against Holland, and permitting him to conquer Flanders and Franche-Comté for France. Madame remained at Dover from May 24 to June 12; she then re-embarked for France, happy in the successful result of her mission; and she arrived at Saint-Germain on the 18th. 'At the age of twenty six,' says Madame de la Fayette, 'she saw herself the link between the two greatest kings of the century; she had in her hands a treaty on which depended the fate of a part of Europe; the pleasure and the importance given by affairs of moment being joined in her with the attractions bestowed by youth and beauty; there was a grace and a sweetness enveloping her whole person that won for her a kind of homage, which must have been the more pleasant in that it was rendered rather to her personality than to her rank.'

Need anything be said of the manners of Monsieur? 'The miracle of firing the heart of this prince,' says Madame de la Fayette, 'was reserved for no woman in the world.' And yet his heart was wonderfully tender! Madame had definitively secured the exile of the Chevalier de Lorraine, the infamous friend of her husband.

Madame died suddenly at St. Cloud, a prey to the most cruel anguish, on the night of the 29th of June 1670, about three o'clock in the morning. Rumours of poison were instantly set afloat, which were not long in gaining strength and currency. They formed the general opinion at Court, in Paris, in the whole of France, in England, Holland, and Spain, where Madame's daughter became queen. Charles II refused to receive the letter in which the Duke of Orleans informed him of his sister's death. 'The Duke of Buckingham, the English ambassador,' wrote Colbert de Croissy, 'is in transports of rage.' The people of London were hardly restrained from violent outbursts against the Frenchmen residing there. The streets rang with the cry of 'Down with the French!' The French embassy had to be protected. Monsieur's second wife, Madame Palatine, was always convinced that Madame had died of poison, and everything tends to show that Louis XIV, at all events in the first moments, shared these suspicions.

In regard to the possible authors of the crime, some accused the Dutch, against whom the Treaty of Dover was directed; others accused Monsieur himself and the Chevalier de Lorraine. In either case, the historical interest of the problem is very great; the popular imagination heightened it through the magnificent commentary with which Bossuet embroidered the death of the beautiful princess; and it has been enhanced by all the efforts made for more than a century past to solve it. 'For fifty years and more,' writes one of the masters of modern erudition, M. Arthur de Boislisle, 'the question has been more closely studied, and the evidence weighed with more care, at least by impartial and serious writers familiar with the documents of Louis XIV's reign or with scientific problems. But it happens that some have abstained from giving a decisive verdict, and others have varied between poison, in which Walckenaer, Paul Lacroix, and François Ravaisson very firmly believed, and death by accident or disease, accepted by Mignet, Loiseleur, and Littré; with the result that the question has become darkened rather than illuminated between conclusions diametrically opposed, but coming from men of equal authority.' Monsieur de Boislisle himself refrains from stating any conclusion, and recently we have Doctor Legué, a specialist, in his interesting book, *Médecins et Empoisonneurs*, devoting a new study to the question, and endeavouring to prove that Madame was poisoned by corrosive sublimate.

Thanks to a minute study of the documents, guided by the work of Monsieur de Boislisle we have just quoted, thanks above all to the skilful guidance of two masters of modern science, we arrive, as will be seen by and by, at an indisputable solution.

I

In accordance with the first principle of historical criticism, it is important at the outset to determine exactly the value of the sources whence we may derive particulars serviceable to our investigation. The sources are divided into three well-marked categories—(1) The reports of the physicians and surgeons; (2) the accounts of the persons who were able to approach Madame in her last moments, or were in a position to hear authoritative descriptions; (3) the official correspondence of the courts of London and Paris.

The first category presents to us five reports of the post-mortem examination:—

(*a*) The official report signed by the fifteen physicians and surgeons, French and English, who were present at the autopsy.

(*b*) The *Account of the Illness, Death, and Autopsy of Madame*, by the Abbé Bourdelot, physician. Bourdelot was one of the French physicians present at the post-mortem.

(*c*) The report of Vallot, physician to the late queen-mother. Vallot was regarded as one of the most eminent physicians of his time. He was present among the French doctors at the autopsy. His report was officially carried to London by the Marshal de Bellefonds.

(*d*) The *Memoir of a Surgeon of the King of England who was present at the Opening of the Body*. This surgeon's name was Alexander Boscher.

(*e*) The account of Hugh Chamberlain, physician-in-ordinary to the King of England, also present at the operation. This document, like the preceding, is exceedingly useful for checking the official report and the report of the French physicians. Some writers have believed that Louis XIV, fearing a rupture with England, dictated the opinion the French physicians were to give. Boscher and Chamberlain were absolutely independent representatives of the English Government.

To these five documents, of unquestionable authenticity, may be added the notice inserted in the *Gazette* of July 5, 1670, which was officially inspired by the Court physicians, and the opinion of the famous Guy Patin, Dean of the Medical School of Paris, though he was not actually present at the autopsy.

In our second category, the narratives of persons who approached Madame in her last moments, or heard authoritative accounts, we must mention prominently the account written by the charming Countess de la Fayette, *The History of Madame Henrietta of England, first wife of Philip of France, Duke of Orleans*. The Countess de la Fayette was attached to the suite of Madame; she never left her during the day on which she died. She has left a simple, precise, and sober account of the short illness, in which every line bears the stamp of truth.

Next to this valuable document must be cited the letter of Bossuet, who was present at the final scene, and the story of Feuillet, canon of St. Cloud, who was with Madame before Bossuet arrived.

The third category comprises the correspondence exchanged between the courts of England and France and their representatives: these would be documents of the greatest value, if their official and diplomatic character had not imposed the greatest reserve on the writers, and even dictated their sentiments. There are first of all the letters of Louis XIV and Hugues de Lionne to Charles II and to Colbert de Croissy, ambassador at London; then, the despatches of Louis and of Hugues de Lionne to Monsieur de Pomponne, ambassador at the Hague; on the English side, five letters addressed by Lord Montagu, ambassador at the French Court, to Lord Arlington, secretary of state to Charles II, and the letters of Lord Arlington to Sir William Temple.

Such are the only documents worthy of credence we have at our disposal for studying the circumstances of the death of Madame, for it is necessary to reject in the most absolute manner the accounts of Saint-Simon and of Monsieur's second wife, Madame Palatine. Chéruel, and more especially Monsieur de Boislisle, have shown the improbabilities and absurdities of these, and we shall not refer to them again. The work of Monsieur de Boislisle is particularly interesting in showing that these two famous narratives had a common source. As to the testimony of d'Argenson, Voltaire, and others, destitute, in the nature of the case, of any authority comparable to that of the authors we have mentioned above—it is unnecessary in the points where it confirms the others; on the points where it contradicts them, it cannot prevail; and on the points where it contains new information, it is dangerous to follow, for we lack any evidence by which to check it. Littré acted judiciously in neglecting these writers when compiling his study on the death of Madame, and the reproach levelled against him by Loiseleur is without justification. On the contrary, it is perhaps to this happy stroke of criticism that Littré owed the success of his argument.

II

We proceed to recount, in the simplest and most precise manner in our power, the circumstances of the death of Madame; and from this narrative alone we shall see emerge one of the facts we intend to establish, namely, that Madame could not have been poisoned.

Henrietta of England, 'more comparable to the jasmine than to the rose, very slender, delicate, slightly round-shouldered—not less pleasing for that—exhausted, not only by four accouchements in rapid succession, but by the fast life then led at Court, was only kept up,' says Monsieur de

Boislisle, 'by that sanguine temperament which is the prerogative of high-strung women.' In 1664 Guy Patin wrote: 'The Duchess of Orleans was taken ill at Villers-Cotterets, and her physicians have prescribed ass's milk.' The presumption is, then, that she suffered from some stomachic disorder. 'The king,' wrote Hugues de Lionne to Colbert de Croissy, 'tells us that more than three years ago she complained of a pain in the side which compelled her to lie flat for three or four hours without finding ease in any posture.' Madame was constantly afflicted with a pain at one fixed spot in the breast. 'She further used to complain,' wrote the Abbé Bourdelot, 'of a cruel burning pain, not in the abdomen, but in the chest.' She was always wanting to vomit. 'Most often she could take only milk for food, and remained in bed for days together.' These facts indicate, as Dr. Le Gendre tells us, that Madame suffered from a chronic inflammation of the stomach, a form of gastritis. The reports of the autopsy show, further, that Madame was afflicted with pulmonary tuberculosis, and it is not rare for these two morbid conditions to co-exist.

During the journey she made in Flanders with the king and Monsieur before her departure for England, the appearance of the young princess caused much alarm. 'She was reduced to living on milk,' writes Madame de la Fayette, 'and retired to her own room as soon as she got out of the coach, and as a rule she went to bed.... One day, when the talk fell on astrology, Monsieur said that it had been foretold that he would have several wives, and judging from the state Madame was in, he was beginning to believe it.'

Madame returned from England on June 18. Her condition had become very much worse. Next day she kept her bed. 'She went into the queen's room,' wrote Mademoiselle de Montpensier, 'like a dressed-up corpse with rouge on its cheeks, and when she went out, everybody, including the queen, said that she had death written on her face.' 'On June 24, 1670,' writes Madame de la Fayette, 'a week after her return from England, Monsieur and she went to St. Cloud. The first day she went there she complained of pains in the side and abdomen, to which she was subject. Nevertheless, as it was extremely hot, she desired to bathe in the river. Monsieur Yvelin, her chief physician, did all he could to prevent her, but in spite of all he said she bathed on Friday the 27th, and on Saturday she was so ill that she did not bathe. I arrived at St. Cloud on Saturday at six o'clock in the evening. I found her in the gardens. She told me that I should think her looking cross, and that she was not at all well. She had supped as usual, and she walked in the moonlight till midnight.' The preceding lines, every detail of which is of great importance, have been neglected by the historians who have concluded she was poisoned.

'On Sunday the 29th, at dinner, Madame ate as usual, and after dinner she lay down on some cushions, as she often did when she was at liberty. She had made me place myself near her,' says Madame de la Fayette, 'so that her head was almost on me. An English painter was painting Monsieur's portrait; we were talking about all sorts of things, and meanwhile she fell asleep. During her nap she changed so considerably that after watching her for a long time I was surprised at it, and thought that her spirit must do a great deal towards adorning her countenance, since it was so pleasant when she was awake and so little attractive when she was asleep. But I was wrong in this reflection, for I had several times seen her sleeping, and had never yet seen her less lovely. When she awoke, she rose from the place where she had been lying, but with so haggard a face that Monsieur was surprised and called my attention to it. She then went away into the drawing-room, where she walked up and down for some time with Boisfranc, Monsieur's treasurer, and while talking to him, complained several times of the pain at her side.'

We are coming to the moment when any poisoning must have taken place; we see already that the mischief was done.

'Monsieur went downstairs to return to Paris. He found Madame de Meckelbourg on the steps, and came up again with her. Madame left Boisfranc and came to Madame de Meckelbourg. As she was speaking to her, Madame de Gamaches brought to her, as well as to me, a glass of chicory water that she had asked for some time before. Madame de Gourdon, her tire-woman, gave it to her. She drank it, and then, replacing the cup on the salver with one hand, she pressed her side with the other, saying, in a tone that betokened severe pain, "Oh! what a dreadful twinge! Oh, what a pain! I can bear it no longer!"

'She reddened in uttering these words, and the next moment turned a livid pallor, which surprised us all; she continued to cry out, and told us to take her away, as she could no longer stand. We took her in our arms; she tottered along half doubled-up; I held her while some one unlaced her. She moaned all the time, and I noticed that she had tears in her eyes. I was amazed and affected by it, for I knew that she was the most patient creature in the world. Kissing the arms I was holding, I said that she was evidently in great pain, and she told me I could not imagine how great. She was put to bed, and as soon as she was there, she cried out more loudly than she had yet done, and threw herself from one side to the other like a person in infinite agony. Some one went off to find her chief physician, Monsieur Esprit; he came, said it was colic, and prescribed the ordinary remedies for such ailments. All the time the pain was dreadful. Madame said that it was much worse than we thought, and that she was dying, and begged some one to go in search of a confessor for her.'

The young princess believed that she was poisoned. A sort of antidote was brought her in the shape of oil and powdered adder, which made her vomit. After some hours of frightful agony, Henrietta of England expired while Bossuet was reciting the last exhortations.

Face to face with death, Madame displayed a greatness of soul to which all who approached her have borne touching testimony. 'Madame was gentle towards Death,' said Bossuet, 'as she had been with all the world. Her great heart was neither embittered nor wrathful against the dread foe. Nor did she face him with proud disdain, but was content to look him in the face without emotion and to welcome him without distress.'

III

This bare narrative of the facts would be sufficient to weaken the opinion of those who believe that the Princess Henrietta died of poison. The following observations will contribute to deprive it of all credit. Writers are unanimously agreed about the fact that Madame could only have been poisoned by the glass of chicory water given her by Madame de Gamaches. Now as soon as suspicions awoke in the mind of Madame and her circle, that is to say, the moment after the drink had been taken, Monsieur ordered some of the water to be given to a dog; Madame Desbordes, the princess's maid, who was heartily devoted to her, told her that she had made the drink, and had herself drunk some of it, and Madame de Meckelbourg also drank some. We are thus bound to acknowledge that the famous chicory water could not have been poisoned. Monsieur J. Lair, with his clear and vigorous mind, has well analysed the scene: 'The decoction of which so many persons had drunk was harmless; it was the cup that ought to have been examined.' 'The details given by Madame de la Fayette and others,' writes Monsieur de Boislisle, 'exclude the idea of poison poured into the glass itself; and indeed Madame Palatine says that what was poisoned was not the water itself, nor the vessel in which it was made, but the cup which was reserved for the princess, and which no one else would have dared to use.'

It is a fact that the seventeenth-century poisoners sought to prepare goblets and silver cups in such a way as to poison the persons who were afterwards to use them. Among the constant friends of La Voisin, La Bosse, La Chéron, and La Vigoureux, the most renowned sorceresses of the period, we find a certain François Belot, one of the king's bodyguard, making a specialty of this, and deriving a comfortable income from it, until the day when this trade led him to the Place de Grève, where he was broken on the wheel on June 10, 1679. His method of procedure was as follows: 'He crammed a toad with arsenic, placed it in a silver goblet, and then, pricking its head, made it urinate, and finally crushed it in the goblet.'

During this pleasant operation he mumbled his wicked charms. 'I know a secret,' said Belot, 'such that in doctoring a cup with a toad and what I put into it, if fifty persons chanced to drink from it afterwards, even if it were washed and rinsed, they would all be done for, and the cup could only be disinfected by throwing it into a hot fire. After having thus poisoned the cup, I should not try it upon a human being, but upon a dog, and I should intrust the cup to nobody.' But it happened that a client of Belot's, being somewhat sceptical, got a dog to drink out of the doctored cup, and found that the animal was not harmed in the least; he even picked a violent quarrel with the magician about the matter, taunting him with the worthlessness of his wares. Belot spoke frankly to the commissioners of the Chambre Ardente: 'I know that the toad cannot do anybody any harm; what I did with the silver cups and trenchers was done solely to get hold of such cups and trenchers.' His skill, nevertheless, enjoyed a very substantial reputation. At the same date the magician Blessis was believed to know how to manipulate mirrors in such a way that any one who looked in them received his deathblow.

These facts seem mere childish folly under scientific investigation. The knowledge people had of poisons in the eighteenth century was limited to arsenic, antimony, and sublimate; it did not enable them so to poison a cup as to cause sudden death to the person using it, without his being aware of the poison at the moment of drinking it. The opinion of Professor Brouardel on this point is explicit; and Dr. Legué, convinced as he is of the poisoning of Madame, admits that the story of the cup can only make any well-informed man smile.

The conclusion is that as Madame could not have been poisoned by the water she drank, or by the cup containing the water, she could not have been poisoned at all.

IV

'Her body was opened,' writes Bossuet, 'among a large concourse of physicians and surgeons and all sorts of people, because, having begun to feel extreme pain when drinking three mouthfuls of chicory water, given her by the dearest and most intimate of her women, she said at once that she was poisoned.' It was with the same idea that the English ambassador attended the operation along with an English physician and surgeon.

After having shown that Madame could not have been poisoned, it remains to settle what disease it was of which she died. Our task is simplified by the marvellous study in which Littré proved that she succumbed to an acute peritonitis, the immediate and inevitable result of the perforation of the stomach by an ulcer. This study, Dr. Paul Le Gendre tells us, is the finest extant example of a retrospective medical demonstration. We have it now under our eyes; but we find it condensed by the pen of the most elegant writer of our time, M. Anatole France, who will allow us to borrow this quotation: 'Littré, an expert in medical observation, does not hesitate to diagnose a simple ulceration of the stomach, which Professor Cruveilhier was the first to describe, and which Madame's physicians could not recognise because they knew nothing about it. It is unquestionable that for some time Madame had been suffering from abdominal pains after her meals. The liquid she took on June 29 brought about the perforation of the ulcerated wall, and this caused the terrible pain in her side and the peritonitis which we have mentioned. The physicians who opened the body found, indeed, that the stomach was pierced with a little hole; but as they could not account for the pathological origin of this hole, they fancied after the event that it had been made inadvertently during the autopsy, "upon which," says the surgeon of the king of England, "I was the only one to insist." The incident is reported as follows by the Abbé Bourdelot: "It happened by misadventure during the dissection that the point of the scalpel made an opening at the top of the ventricle, and many of the gentlemen asked how it came about. The surgeon said that he had done it by accident, and Monsieur Vallot said that he had seen when the cut was made."'

Littré objects, with reason, that it is difficult to make inadvertently an incision with the point of a pair of scissors—there is no question of a scalpel—in a tough and distended membrane like the stomach during an autopsy. The illusion of the physicians present at the operation is the more easily explained because in that lesion, as it is now known, the edges of the opening are perfectly clean and sharp, very regular, so that the hole seems to have been made artificially. Jaccoud points out 'the very sharp delimitation of the ulcer, the absence of inflammation, and of peripheral suppuration.' 'The section of the tissues,' writes Monsieur Bouveret, 'is so clean that, to adopt a classical comparison, the ulcer appears as though cut out with a punch.' It varies in dimensions from the size of a lentil to that of a five-franc piece.

M. Anatole France admirably explains the state of mind of the physicians who drew up the report of the autopsy. 'The French physicians were afraid of finding in the viscera of the princess indications of a crime which might throw suspicion on the royal family. They dreaded even everything which lent itself to doubt, and thereby to malevolence. Knowing that the least uncertainty as to the cause of death or the condition of the corpse would be interpreted by the public in a sense that would ruin them, they had reasons of self-interest and the zeal of fear to urge them to explain everything. Now, in their inability to connect with a normal pathological type a lesion unknown to them all, and perhaps suspicious to some, it was much to their advantage to explain this enigmatical wound as an accident during the autopsy. And we can understand their believing what they wished to believe. The English surgeons, as ignorant as they, accepted their conclusion in default of a better.' 'The fact is,' says Littré in conclusion, 'that they were bound to find a hole, and they did find it. All dispute was silenced in the presence of three things: the sudden attack, the peritonitis, and the presence of oil ['and of bile,' adds Dr. Le Gendre] which the reports of the autopsy show to have been in the lower bowel.' In the lower bowel was found, indeed, a substance which the reports of the French physicians describe as 'fat like oil.'[13] It was, in fact, oil—the oil which Madame had drunk as an antidote, and which had been discharged from the stomach.

Further, even supposing, against all probability, that the hole had actually been made accidentally by young Félix, who was the operator, all the details of Madame's health known before death, and the details revealed by the autopsy, are so conclusive in favour of the diagnosis of a simple ulcer ending in perforation, that we should be led to the admission that there must have existed, in another part of the wall of the stomach, another small hole which escaped the notice of the physicians and surgeons present at the autopsy. There would have been nothing surprising in this, for their attention was not directed to this point. It might even be supposed that the scissors of Félix, if they had really cut the wall of the stomach by inadvertence, only increased the size of the natural perforation already existing. Allowance must indeed be made for the state of putrid softening in which the organs are bound to have been, the corpse having remained exposed all through a day of intense heat.

'To sum up, before June 29, there were gastric pains caused by ulceration; on the 29th, bursting of the ulcer and acute peritonitis.' Peritonitis is distinctly indicated by the reports. Such are the conclusions of Littré: Dr. Paul Le Gendre, a most competent authority, unhesitatingly confirms them, as also does Professor Brouardel, who writes as follows: 'Admitting ulceration of the stomach, all the phenomena supervene with classic exactitude.'

If we refer to the works of the celebrated Cruveilhier, who was the first to describe simple ulcers, we find by an interesting coincidence, in the very case he presents as a type, the closest correspondence with the illness of Madame, and a fresh proof of the soundness of Littré's opinion.

'Now since the complications following perforation of the stomach and rapidly causing death,' writes Cruveilhier, 'supervene suddenly, and sometimes directly after taking food or drink, the question of poison has been raised pretty often. I have never seen a more remarkable case in this respect than that of a coalman, aged twenty-three, and of an athletic vigour, who, carrying a sack of coal, stopped at an inn and drank a glass of wine. He went on his way; but a few minutes afterwards was seized with horrible pains, was attended first at his own house, then carried dying to the hospital of the Faubourg Saint-Denis; his case showed every indication of peritonitis through perforation, and he died three hours after his admission to the hospital, in full consciousness. I was able to get from his own lips the valuable information that he had been suffering from his stomach for several months, and that digesting his food was always painful. The Coal-dealers' Society, convinced that their comrade was the victim of poison, and that the agent of the poisoning was the glass of wine taken immediately before he was attacked by these symptoms, decided to bring an indictment against the wine-merchant, and with this end required the autopsy to be made in presence of a deputation from their body. It was a case of spontaneous perforation through a simple ulcer in the stomach.'

The 'estimate' of Littré (to use the phrase he himself uses to describe his work) is thus confirmed in every way. Loiseleur thought fit to object the rarity of the case. That is no argument: the case may be rare and yet have been that of Madame. And besides, Loiseleur makes too much of its rarity. Brinton estimates that perforation of the stomach in cases of simple ulcer occurs in thirteen per cent., and that it is most common in women under thirty. Madame was twenty-six.

Loiseleur admits peritonitis, but thinks it was inflammation supervening on a chill. 'Why,' he writes, 'does Littré pass by in absolute silence the last words in the statement of Madame de la Fayette, quite as grave and significant as the first?—"As it was extremely warm, she wished to bathe in the river. Monsieur Yvelin, her chief physician, did all he could to prevent her; but in spite of all he said, she bathed on Friday, and on Saturday was so ill that she did not bathe," and further on: "She walked in the moonlight until midnight."' There is only one drawback to Monsieur Loiseleur's theory, but that is a serious one: peritonitis as an original malady, and especially peritonitis through chill, which Loiseleur wishes to substitute for the disease diagnosed by Cruveilhier and Littré, is no longer recognised by modern science. 'The last cases which were thought to be of this kind,' says Dr. Paul Le Gendre, 'were perforations of the appendix.'

Let us come lastly to the work of Dr. Legué, *Médecins et Empoisonneurs*, the most important part of which is occupied with a minute study of the circumstances surrounding the death of Madame. Monsieur Legué's conclusion is, poisoning by sublimate poured into the famous chicory water. His study is interesting, like the whole book, but his conclusions crumble away under the following considerations:—

1. Professor Brouardel writes: 'If the chicory water had contained the smallest dose of sublimate, Madame would have pushed the glass from her after the first sip. Sublimate has a revolting taste. In the medicinal dose (one gramme to a litre) the taste is atrocious.'

Madame had been taking chicory water for several days in the evening, and this evening she drank it as usual.

2. 'To kill a person,' adds Professor Brouardel, 'at least ten or fifteen centigrammes are necessary. This dose corresponds to a quantity of solution representing about 200 grammes of liquid. It seems impossible for any one to imbibe that without being stopped by its horrid taste.'

Madame certainly did not drink 200 grammes of her chicory water; she took a few sips only.

3. 'Poisoning by sublimate,' writes the professor, 'produces lesions of the abdominal mucous membrane, which could not have escaped the notice of the physicians who made the autopsy.'

We have five accounts of the autopsy, which are unanimous in stating that the stomach, except for the little hole of which we have spoken, was in a good condition.

4. The facts on which Dr. Legué relies for his diagnosis of poison by sublimate, and which he borrows from the account of the Abbé Bourdelot, occurred, not after the drinking of the cup of chicory water, but before. In transcribing the account in question, Monsieur Legué has inadvertently omitted the passage: 'There is indication of the bile having been accumulating for a long time,' where it may be clearly seen from the following lines that the author is speaking of a state long before the fatal attack.

Thus Monsieur Legué's argument is in no way sustained.

The historian may remark, finally, that Madame's daughter, Marie Louise, the young Queen of Spain, died in 1689, almost at the same age as her mother, after drinking a glass of iced milk, and on this occasion also rumours of poison spread abroad. When Charles II, Madame's brother, died somewhat suddenly, there was more talk of poison; and when the granddaughter of Madame, the young and charming Duchess of Burgundy, was stricken with the disease which carried her off, people believed that she too had been poisoned. In earlier days, when Madame's mother, Henrietta Maria of France, widow of Charles I, died on September 10, 1669, at her country house of Colombes, her physician Vallot had been accused of accidentally poisoning her by giving her pills chiefly composed of opium.

Thanks to the assistance of eminent masters like Professor Brouardel and Dr. Paul Le Gendre, and armed historically with the learned investigations of M. Arthur de Boislisle, we have been fortunate in resuscitating the admirable study of Littré in all its striking accuracy. The great writer concludes with an eloquent page, a hymn of triumph in honour of modern science, 'which might perhaps have kept Madame in that great place she filled so well.' We will end with the same observation that we placed at the end of our study of the Iron Mask,[14] in which we showed how the solution was indicated at least a century ago, and remarked that, in these very problems which are regarded as insoluble, history, handled with rigour and precision, gives conclusions as certain as those of the exact sciences.

RACINE AND THE POISONS QUESTION

MONSIEUR LARROUMET'S book on Racine in the *Grands Ecrivains Français* series is a charming little work. In the first part he studies the poet's life, and shows very accurately the influence exercised on his art by the *milieu* in which he lived. In the second part he studies Racine's poetics with great ingenuity. The very style of M. Larroumet, eminently refined and sober—we might call it pearl-grey in tone—with little flaws here and there which, to our mind, enhance its piquancy, is perfectly adapted to the author he is analysing. We get a clear picture of what manner of man Racine was—sensitive and refined, all delicacy and decorum. M. Larroumet, it is well known, excels in bringing vividly before us the dwellings and the furniture of our great writers, according to inventories made after their decease. In the case of Racine he achieves another success, in the happiest manner. His picture of the famous poet's family life, after he had renounced the stage, is delightful:—

'In the midst of this family, which reproduced in charming variety the traits of his own sensitive and restless nature, Racine practised all the virtues of a good father. He became a child again with his Babet, Fanchon, Madelon, Nanette, and Lionval; the two eldest alone, boy and girl, did not bear these diminutives, out of respect for the rights of seniority. He preferred the happiness springing from their society to courting the great.

'One day he had returned from Versailles, where he had gone to pay his respects, when a squire of the Duke's brought him an invitation to dinner for the same evening. "I shall not have the honour of dining with him," he said; "I have not seen my wife and children for more than a week, and they are looking forward to a treat in eating a very fine carp with me to-day; I cannot give up my dinner with them." And he had the carp brought up, adding: "Decide yourself if I can help dining to-day with these poor children, who have made up their minds to regale me to-day, and would have no more pleasure if they ate this dish without me. I beg you to plead this reason forcibly with his Serene Highness."'

Racine, as we know, after giving up writing for the theatre, subsided into the most remarkable piety. But here again is a charming trait: 'I remember,' says Louis Racine, 'processions in which my sisters were the clergy, I was the rector, and the author of *Athalie*, singing with us, carried the cross.' And the inseparable figure of the excellent Boileau, who had then become as deaf as a post, appears close by: 'Monsieur Despréaux,'[15] writes Racine to his son Jean Baptiste, 'entertained us in the best of fashions; then he took Lionval and Madelon to the Bois de Boulogne, joking with them, and telling them that he meant to lose them. He did not hear a word of what the poor children said to him.'

But before becoming this model paterfamilias, this pattern of piety and virtue, Racine had spent an eminently brilliant and passionate youth. Everybody knows that Du Parc and Champmeslé[16] were not content with merely playing in his pieces.

The amours of Racine and Mademoiselle Du Parc had a terrible development in 1679, which was one of the reasons, if not the principal and the determining reason, of the resolution then taken by the poet to abandon the career of dramatic author. M. Larroumet recalls this page in his life in the following terms:—

'The mysterious poison affair was being unravelled before the Chambre Ardente. On November 21, 1679, one of the prisoners, La Voisin, brought Racine into the case. She declared that "Racine, having secretly espoused Du Parc, was jealous of everybody, and particularly of her, La Voisin, with whom he was much offended, and that he had made away with her by poison on account of his extreme jealousy; and that during Du Parc's illness, Racine never left her bedside, that he drew a valuable diamond from her finger, and had also stolen the jewels and principal effects of Du Parc, which were worth a great deal of money." This is assuredly nothing but the abominable invention of a ruined woman,' adds M. Larroumet, 'one of those calumnies which malice, corruption, and greed give rise to in the entourage of women of gallantry. Racine had been compelled to forbid his mistress to receive La Voisin. From this arose her furious wrath, and, eleven years afterwards, she tried to avenge herself by implicating the poet in a formidable accusation. Proofs she gave none, and the proceedings of the affair, published in the *Archives de la Bastille*, contain no trace of any. However, a letter written on January 11, 1680, by Louvois to Bazin de Bezons, ends thus: "The orders of the king necessary for the arrest of Racine will be sent to you whenever you ask for them." It is impossible to doubt that the Racine in question was the poet. But no arrest was made. Racine had been able to clear himself in the eyes of Louvois and the king.'

This episode in the life of the great poet is worthy of arresting our attention, so much the more because it was perhaps the cause of his abandonment, to be for ever regretted, of a career on which he had thrown the brightest lustre.

It was neither Louvois nor Louis XIV who suppressed the *lettre de cachet* with which the deposition of La Voisin had threatened Racine. Bazin de Bezons, a commissioner of the Chambre Ardente and member of the

Academy, determined to spare his colleague the affront of an arrest in such circumstances, and thought he might well wait until the denunciations of La Voisin were confirmed from another source.

Racine, as a matter of fact, had been the lover of Du Parc, whose maiden name was Marguerite Thérèse de Gorla, daughter of a surgeon of Lyons. La Voisin knew her very intimately, and called her her 'gossip.'

Here follows, word for word, the part of the celebrated examination of La Voisin on November 21, 1679, so far as it relates to Racine:—

'Who made her acquainted with Du Parc, comedian?

'She had known her for fourteen years. They were very good friends together, and she knew all her affairs during that time. She had for some time had the intention of declaring to us that Du Parc must have been poisoned, and that Jean Racine was suspected. The rumour was strong. What more especially gave rise to the presumption was that Racine had always prevented her, who was the good friend of Du Parc, from seeing her during the whole course of the illness of which she died, although Du Parc constantly asked for her; but although she went to see her, they had never been willing to let her in, and this was by order of Racine, as she learnt from the stepmother of Du Parc, whose name was Mademoiselle de Gorla, and from Du Parc's daughters, who are at the Hôtel de Soissons, and informed her that Racine was the cause of their misfortune.

'Asked if he had ever proposed to her to do away with Du Parc by poison.

'The proposal would have been well received.

'Asked if she was not aware that application had been made to Delagrange for the same purpose.

'She knew nothing about that.

'Asked if she did not know a lame actor.

'Yes, Béjart, whom she had only seen twice.

'Asked if Béjart had not some spite against Du Parc.

'No; and what she knew about Racine she obtained first from Mademoiselle de Gorla.

'Asked what De Gorla said to her, and strictly cross-examined.

'De Gorla told her that Racine, having secretly espoused Du Parc [here follows a repetition of the statement already made]; that she (Du Parc) had not even been allowed to speak to Manon, her maid, who is a midwife, though she asked for Manon and got some one to write asking her to come to Paris to see her, as well as La Voisin herself.

'Asked if De Gorla told her the manner in which the poisoning had been carried out, and who had been made use of in the matter.

'No.'

Such were the declarations of La Voisin before the commissioners of the Chambre Ardente. She repeated them exactly in her final examination before the judges: 'She had known Mademoiselle Du Parc, the actress; had been a friend of hers for fourteen years; her stepmother, named De Gorla, had told her that Racine had poisoned her, and she only knew of Du Parc's death when she saw the body at the door on the way to burial.'

Finally, in the anguish of torture, La Voisin maintained her declarations.

'Asked if she knew nothing more concerning what she had said at the trial about the poisoning of Du Parc.

'She had told the truth in all that she had said on the subject.'

M. Larroumet gaily and gracefully flings these declarations overboard as 'an abominable invention of a ruined woman.' We know La Voisin from what has already been said about her above. It is inconceivable that such a creature should have nursed a grievance against Racine for not having allowed her to reach his sick mistress, to such an extent as to fabricate against him, eleven years later, so monstrous an accusation. This hypothesis is so much the more unlikely in that, if La Voisin had wanted to ruin Racine by her charges, she would have formulated precise and direct complaints against him; while she, as a matter of fact, only repeated gossip she had heard. Then, too, Du Parc's daughters were still alive, and it would have been easy to confront them with the sorceress.

The examinations to which La Voisin was subjected were very numerous. They brought out innumerable details on a multitude of crimes, in which a very large number of people was implicated. There were many confrontations. The declarations of the terrible sorceress were submitted to careful investigation by examining magistrates like Nicolas de la Reynie. All her declarations were found to be accurate.

We have seen that, far from inventing imaginary charges for the purpose of implicating in her own case people of high position, and so saving herself (as some historians have insinuated), La Voisin endeavoured to keep silence about the crimes of her clients—a curious piece of professional discretion. And we venture to say that if she had declared before the judges that she had given Racine poison to get rid of Du Parc, we should have unhesitatingly believed her. But she did not say anything of the kind. She declared simply that, in Du Parc's immediate circle, it was the conviction that the actress had been poisoned by her lover, and that, throughout her illness, he had prevented La Voisin from approaching the bed, as well as Manon, her maid, 'who was a midwife.'

It is further important to note—and this observation has not been made by any historian—that the belief in Racine's having poisoned Du Parc was shared by more than one prisoner before the Chambre Ardente. La Voisin was not the only one to make the accusation before the judges, as the following question put by one of the magistrates clearly shows:

'Asked if she was not aware that application had been made to Delagrange (a sorceress and poisoner like herself) for the same purpose (the poisoning of Du Parc by Racine).'

A great part of the records of the Chambre Ardente having been destroyed, as we have shown, we have no trace of the examination to which the magistrate here alluded. Nevertheless it is testimony which cannot be gainsaid.

Such are the only documents in the great poison case in which Racine is mentioned. Is it possible to derive any positive conclusions from them?

The circumstances surrounding the death certainly appeared suspicious to the family of the actress, and Racine was pointed at. The poet had stationed himself at the bedside as a custodian rather than a nurse. He prevented La Voisin, the sorceress, midwife, and procurer of abortion, from approaching, and likewise Manon, also a midwife, and this in defiance of the desire formally expressed by Du Parc. Why did the poet, contrary to the wishes of the sick woman, prevent these women from attending her? Du Parc was his mistress. Dr. Legué quotes the testimony of Boileau, who was closely connected with Du Parc, stating that she died as a result of childbirth. The chronicler Robinet describes Racine as following 'more dead than alive' in the funeral procession. The opinion expressed by Dr. Legué that Du Parc died through an illegal operation is not unlikely. In such matters it is never possible to speak with assurance, and when so great a personality as Racine is concerned, one is bound to maintain the greatest reserve. This operation, if it took place, brought on peritonitis, which, as in the case of Henrietta of England, gave rise to suspicions of poison. We have seen that abortions were at that time of frequent occurrence in Paris.

Remorse for this crime would explain the amazing resolution to renounce the theatre taken by Racine at the age of thirty-eight, in the fulness of strength, at the height of his talent, in the heyday of success. It would explain also the austerity and excess of his devoutness after this singular conversion, and the horror he conceived for an art to which he owed his glory and his fortune.

Another question suggests itself, which we should like equally to be able to solve with more certainty. Racine had the most intimate relations with Du Parc, as the latter had with La Voisin. In 1679, the year in which the great poisoning matter came to light, *Phèdre* appeared. Is it rash to suppose that, through his conversations with Du Parc, La Voisin's confidante, the poet with his keen observation had seen the features of the passion-tost marchionesses, criminals for love, who had been the clients of the sorceresses, and that from these fleeting suggestions he had succeeded in reconstructing their whole characters?

'Imagine,' writes Monsieur Brunetière, 'Racine's agitation when this case became public. At Paris, in the heart of Paris—the Paris of Louis XIV—in the Rue Verdelet or the Rue Michel-Lecomte, Orestes was assassinating Pyrrhus, Roxane was selling herself to some witch to secure the love of Bajazet or the death of Attalide; the famous Locusta was not an invention of Tacitus, and every day some Phèdre was poisoning some Hippolyte. And all these horrors were what he, Racine, had been for ten years toiling to envelop and to disguise, as it were, with the charm of his verse—murder and lust! adultery and incest! the delirium of the senses! the madness of homicide! This was what for ten years he had been endeavouring to win plaudits for, and when a Hermione or a Nero issued from the Hôtel de Bourgogne[17] intent on committing the crime they had seen glorified under their eyes—what, was it this that he called his glory! O shame and agony and remorse! And from the moment that such a question started up before the conscience of such a man, how think you he could have answered but by quitting the stage? The truth even of his own art rose up against him. What brought his pictures into condemnation was just their accent of truth!'

THE 'DEVINERESSE'

LA DEVINERESSE, a fairy comedy by Donneau de Visé and Thomas Corneille—the latter is usually called by his contemporaries Corneille de Lisle—was represented at Paris in 1679, the year of the great poison case.

In his reports to the king and the Secretaries of State Nicolas de la Reynie insisted on the necessity, not only of punishing the guilty, but of preventing the spread and, if possible, the recurrence of crimes like those which had been brought to light. We have shown how he had drawn up, in collaboration with Colbert, the decree registered in the Parlement on August 31, 1682, by which the magicians were expelled from France, and by which, more especially, the making and the sale of poisons necessary in medicine and in trade were placed under rigorous regulations. This was a masterly work: as we have mentioned, these regulations are in force to this day, after the lapse of two centuries.

La Reynie thought that it was advisable, apart from these preventive measures, to put the public on their guard against the dangerous infatuation which had thrown so many pretty and passionate women body and soul into the hands of the fortune-tellers. Let us recall the declarations of one of the latter: 'Persons who look into the hand are the ruin of all women, women of quality as well as others, because their weakness is soon found out, and when discovered is taken advantage of, and they are driven to whatever length the witches please.' As lieutenant of police La Reynie had a general control of the theatres; he revised and censored the manuscripts of the playwrights; he was in constant touch with them. He was the friend of more than one writer of talent, for the magistrate was doubled in him with the refined and delightful man of letters, who had both delicate taste and an excellent library. In this year 1679 he had particularly close relations with Donneau de Visé, founder and editor of the *Mercure galant*, and assuredly one of the most curious figures in our literary history. Boursault had just written his witty comedy, also entitled the *Mercure galant*, in which he directed lively and incisive satire upon the journalism then at its dawn, which had already taken, under the influence of Donneau de Visé, many of the characteristics of modern journalism.

The *Mercure*, said Boursault, is a delightful thing:—

'On y trouve de tout, fable, histoire, vers, prose,
Sièges, combats, procès, mort, mariage, amour,
Nouvelles de Province et nouvelles de Cour.'

Visé begged La Reynie not to authorise the representation of the piece under the same title as the journal; La Reynie acquiesced, and Boursault, putting a good face on the matter, called his piece *La Comédie sans titre*. Moreover, Visé was in high favour at Court. When Louis XIV saw the success of the *Mercure*, he hastened to award the editor-in-chief a pension of 500 crowns, gave him apartments in the Louvre, and appointed him his historiographer. Visé's pen became an accommodating tool.

Donneau de Visé was not only a journalist; he was a dramatic author, and as a dramatic author he was, as he was in journalism, very modern. He had found means of achieving a noisy notoriety by beginning with an extremely violent attack on Corneille and Molière. Against the latter he composed his comedy *Zélinde, ou la véritable critique de l'Echole des Femmes et la critique de la critique*, in which he has left a portrait of the poet that has become famous, and which is, in our eyes, not a criticism but a splendid eulogy. 'I came down,' says a lace merchant; 'Elomire [an anagram on Molière] did not say a single word. I found him leaning up against my shop in the attitude of a man in a dream. He had his eyes fixed on three or four persons of quality who were bargaining for lace; he appeared attentive to their words, and seemed by the movement of his eyes to be scanning the depths of their souls to see there what they did not say.'

La Reynie thought of utilising the talent and the notoriety of the dramatic author, and, not satisfied with granting him what he asked in regard to the title of Boursault's comedy, he gave him in addition the subject for a piece which was destined to obtain the greatest success. To prove to demonstration in Paris, by means of a play to which the public, excited by the great poison case, would flock in crowds, that the pretended skill of magicians and sorceresses was only deception and trickery, seemed assuredly the best way to dissuade the ingenuous mob from dealing with them. From this idea issued *La Devineresse ou les Faux enchantements*, a comedy represented for the first time in Paris by the king's company on November 19, 1679, and published in the following February. We have mentioned that Donneau de Visé was one of the pioneers of the modern literary life, and *La Devineresse* will be a fresh proof of the assertion. Let us note first that Visé was the father of a literary custom which is in these days highly popular, collaboration. One of the masters of dramatic criticism, Edouard Thierry, writes on this subject: 'Collaboration, an unfamiliar term which existed at most as a term in jurisprudence, was nevertheless not absolutely unknown at the theatre. There had been the *Psyche* at the Palais-Royal, completed by Pierre Corneille on the plan and under the direction of Molière; but this was considered only as work done to order; it belonged in the end to the person who hired the worker. There had been the *Plaideurs* of Racine, and some other successful parodies, composed by several hands, it was said; but this was only an amusement, a literary picnic of gay wits who stimulated each other to satire; nobody up to that time had thought of raising the game to the level of an industry.' From the very first, collaboration as a business gave results which exceeded the most sanguine hopes. Visé, who had made his peace with the elder Corneille, entered into partnership with his younger brother. This Thomas Corneille, who was a remarkable vaudeville-writer and also a remarkable scholar, a member of the Academy of Inscriptions and Belles-Lettres, has been unjustly thrown into the shade by the glory of his elder brother.

La Devineresse was not merely a modern piece in respect of this new trick of collaboration; it was the origin and doubtless the model of those spectacular pieces, with shifting scenery and mechanical effects, which give the Châtelet its success to-day. And we shall find, not only that the idea sprang from this, but that the comedy contains scenes and stage business which have come down to us in direct succession through a line of such pieces—such as the talking headless man, the dismembered man whose limbs rearrange themselves spontaneously, dropsy passing from one subject to another, the fairy, wizard or devil who comes into a room through the wall.

Finally, the *Devineresse* must occupy a select place in the annals of the modern stage from the manner in which the authors managed to float it. One of them, Donneau de Visé, was a journalist, and consequently a master of the advertising art. He had the idea, among others, of getting up for 1680 an almanac of the *Devineresse*, in which there was a large engraved plate representing the principal scenes in the piece, the features of the spectacle, grouped around a monstrous satanic figure; these of course were the principal tricks in false magic performed by the sorceress and her mate. These pictures are still in existence,[18] and present to our eyes a curious representation, not only of the theatrical scenes of the eighteenth century, but also of the interior of the houses in which the sorceresses received their clients. These circumstances, together with the striking actuality and the wit of the authors, secured to the *Devineresse* an unprecedented success, both financially and in arousing the curiosity of the public. All Paris ran to see it. Its representations extended over five months, and, what in those days appeared remarkable, it ran for forty-seven nights in succession; the first eighteen performances brought in double the usual receipts. Seconded by the skill and talent of the authors, the lieutenant of police had attained his end.

The fortune-teller who is the chief character in the piece was none other than La Voisin, whose name Corneille and Visé slightly disguised in calling their sorceress Madame Jobin. In the comedy are to be found echoes of the replies made by the sorceress before the commissioners of the

Chambre Ardente, a fact which indicates the share of La Reynie. The principal ally of La Voisin was called Du Buisson, that of Madame Jobin is called Du Clos. Their practices are the same, but turned to ridicule by the authors, who make their Madame Jobin a mere schemer with no other idea than to snap up the crown-pieces of the public. In the essentials of the character we are thus very far from the terrible sorceress of Villeneuve-sur-Gravois.

In the course of the second scene of the second act, Madame Jobin explains to her brother what her art consists in.

'This is what the majority of men are. They swallow all the stupidities retailed to them, and when once they have let themselves go, nothing is capable of undeceiving them. See, my brother, Paris is the place in the world where there are most clever people and also most dupes. The sorceries I am accused of, and other things which would appear still more supernatural, want a lively imagination to invent them and skill to make use of them. It is through these that people have belief in us, and magic and devils have nothing to do with it. The fright people get into who are shown this sort of thing blinds them enough to prevent them from seeing they are deceived. As to my meddling with fortune-telling, as you will be told, that is an art in which the thousand folk who put themselves every day in our hands make our information easy to get at. Besides, chance accounts for the greater part of our success in this line. All you want is presence of mind, and boldness and intrigue, to know the world, to have people in your houses, to note carefully things that happen, to get information on their little love affairs, and especially to say a good many things when any one comes to consult you. There is always one of them true, and two or three, said quite haphazard, are enough to give you a vogue. After that it will be of no good to say that you know nothing; no one will believe you, and, good or evil, they make you talk.'

The comedy itself is far from being without merit. You will not see in it, to be sure, the breadth and the sureness of touch of that Molière whom Visé had so much ridiculed, and the pleasure one may find in reading it is spoilt by the feeling that Molière would have made so much more of such a subject, in which so many laughable and so many moving things are concentrated. Nevertheless, the majority of modern extravaganzas would have to yield in many respects to the *Devineresse*, as regards both construction and literary merit. In the course of the preface to the published edition of their piece, the authors are careful to speak of the famous rules ascribed to Aristotle without which no dramatic piece could be constructed in the time of Racine and Boileau. And in fact Visé and Corneille did observe them—these three famous unities of time, place, and action. In an extravaganza, mark! That, assuredly, is what an author of our day would consider the most extravagant feature of their work.

The preface states the subject of the comedy: 'A woman mad after the sorceresses, a lover interested in opening her eyes about them, and a rival who wishes to prevent their marriage, form a subject which opens the plot in the first act, a plot only unravelled in the last act by the unmasking of the false devil. The other actors, or at least a part of them, are envoys of one or other of the two interested persons, who, by the reports they give, augment the credulity of the countess or make the marquis believe still more firmly that the sorceress is a knave. Thus these characters cannot be regarded as unnecessary. It is true that there are some who, knowing neither the countess nor the marquis, only consult Madame Jobin on their own behalf; but, being as famous as she is here depicted, was it likely that during twenty-four hours there only came to her persons who knew one another or furthered the principal action?'

From the outset the comedy is well constructed, and the character of the persons comes out clearly. The seasoning of the dialogue is a little strong, indeed; but the wit springs always from an acute and delicate power of observation. We may mention the scene in which the sorceress, who easily dupes persons of cultivated mind and even those who never relax their vigilance, is utterly nonplussed by the primitive simple-mindedness of a village girl. The dénouement is brought about by the presence of mind of the marquis, who seeks to undeceive the countess whom he loves. The sorceress has foretold frightful misfortunes to the countess if she should marry the marquis, being paid for so doing by a Madame Noblet who has fallen deeply in love with the latter. The marquis, armed with a pistol, springs at the throat of a devil whom the sorceress has summoned through the wall. The devil falls on his knees: 'Mercy, sir; I am a good devil!'

It remains to inquire whether the lieutenant of police had as much success as the authors of the piece; that is, whether the practices he wished to extirpate in France disappeared under his efforts. La Reynie did succeed, as much as he could hope, in the struggle he had undertaken against the poisoners. Magic, however, was a hardy plant. 'You would never believe how desperately silly they are at Paris,' wrote Madame Palatine on October 8, 1701. 'Everybody is anxious to become an adept in the art of invoking spirits and other devilries.' Black masses were again said in the outskirts of Paris, in circumstances so horrible that 'a beggar girl aged thirteen years, who had been taken there, died of fright': she was buried in her clothes by sub-deacon Sebault, and Guignard, curé of Notre Dame de Bourges, who had said the monstrous office. And according to M. Huysmans, black masses are said to this very day.

When, two thousand years before our era, the Chaldean mages and the high priests of Egypt on clear nights pierced the starry sky with their patient gaze, did they read there that after thirty centuries a grave magistrate and chief of police would fight their descendants by means of a fairy extravaganza, with trap-doors and puns and transformation scenes?

FOOTNOTES:

[1] As the king's eldest brother was called.

[2] At present 12 Rue Charles V. The house is now occupied by the nursing sisterhood of the Bon-Secours.

[3] [The then law courts of Paris.]

[4] [The supreme judicial tribunal of France.]

[5] [The criminal court.]

[6] [The assassin of Henry of Navarre.]

[7]

['into a sea profound
Where flowed earth's metals in a molten mass,
Would tinge and dye the whole in sunbright gold.']

[8] [In the original, a play on the double meaning of *argent*—'silver' and 'money.']

[9] [Second wife of 'Monsieur,' the king's brother.]

[10] ['To share with Jupiter is no whit dishonouring.']

[11] [Madame de Montespan.]

[12] Written in collaboration with Professor Paul Brouardel, Dean of the Faculty of Medicine at Paris, and Doctor Paul le Gendre, physician to the Tenon infirmary.

[13] The report of Chamberlain, the English physician, says distinctly that it was oil. 'The lower bowel was full of a bilious humour, with oil floating upon it' (Mrs. Everett-Green's *Lives of the Princesses of England*, vi. 589). This observation is important because Littré's opinion has been disputed by Dr. Legué. 'Littré maintains that the physicians noticed the presence of oil; but that is because he strains an equivocal phrase in the report of the autopsy—"full to its utmost capacity of a sanious, putrid, yellowish, watery substance, *fat like oil.*" Frankly, is this not giving to the text a signification which never entered into the mind of the physicians?' (*Médecins et Empoisonneurs*, pp. 255, 256.) Neither Dr. Legué nor Littré, however, knew the English reports published by Mrs. Everett-Green.

[14] *Legends of the Bastille*, p. 146.

[15] [Boileau.]

[16] [Two of the most famous actresses of the time.]

[17] [The theatre so called.]

[18] In a copy of the *Devineresse* in the Arsenal Library. There are others, a little different, in the large folio collection of almanacs in the print department of the National Library.

Milton Keynes UK
Ingram Content Group UK Ltd.
UKHW030625061024
449204UK00004B/324

9 789362 095084